Deceptive Communication

Gerald R. Miller
James B. Stiff

302.
2
MIL

Sage Series

Interpersonal Communication 14

SAGE Publications
International Educational and Professional Publisher
Newbury Park   London   New Delhi

For information address:

SAGE Publications, Inc.
2455 Teller Road
Newbury Park, California 91320

SAGE Publications Ltd.
6 Bonhill Street
London EC2A 4PU
United Kingdom

SAGE Publications India Pvt. Ltd.
M-32 Market
Greater Kailash I
New Delhi 110 048 India

Printed in the United States of America

Library of Congress Cataloging-in-Publication Data

Miller, Gerald R.
    Deceptive Communication / Gerald R. Miller, James B. Stiff.
        p. cm. — (Sage series in interpersonal communication : v. 14)
    Includes bibliographical references and index.
    ISBN 0-8039-3484-X. — ISBN 0-8039-3485-8 (pbk.)
    1. Deception. 2. Interpersonal communication. I. Stiff, James
B. (James Brian) II. Title. III. Series.
    BF637.D42M55   1993
    153.6—dc20   93-15520

93 94 95 96 97 10 9 8 7 6 5 4 3 2 1

Sage Production Editor: Astrid Virding

Contents

Series Editor's Introduction   vii
  Mark L. Knapp

Foreword   ix

1. Deceptive Communication in
   Late 20th Century Society   1

2. Conceptualizing and Defining
   Deceptive Communication   16

3. Investigating Deceptive Communication   32

4. Characteristics of Deceptive Behavior   50

5. Misjudging Veracity:
   The Inaccuracy of Human Lie Detectors   68

6. Factors Influencing
   the Judgments of Veracity   82

7. Challenges for Future Research   102

References   118

Author Index   125

Subject Index   128

About the Authors   131

Series Editor's Introduction

To say this book addresses one of the most significant and pervasive social phenomena of our age is not hyperbole. Lying and deception have become staple social products. They are omnipresent. Standing in the checkout line of your local supermarket, you may read the tabloid headline, "I Had Bigfoot's Baby"; turning on your TV set, you hear about a tax increase from a politician who campaigned on the promise: "Read my lips, no new taxes"; applying for a job, you learn you have to take a polygraph test as a condition of employment; reading the newspaper, you find new laws have been passed to protect you against misleading practices by advertisers, retailers, and money lenders. And shortly after you questioned the veracity of a comment made by your spouse, you sit down with your daughter and confidently assure her that Santa Claus will be coming down the chimney with his bag of presents while his reindeer wait patiently for him on the roof.

But the subject of this book is more than a treatise on an important social issue; it is a book that goes to the very heart of communication studies. The social act of deceiving others inevitably draws attention to a fundamental process involved in communicating effectively—that is, the packaging of information for a specific audience in a specific situation with the purpose of eliciting desired responses. Whenever communication scholars consider the act of lying and/or deception, it forces them to reflect on the complex interconnections and distinctions associated with "effective communication strategies" and "lies." This book, then, should be of particular interest to those who study persuasion, communication competence, and communication as it interfaces with relationships. Those who study nonverbal behavior will also want to read this book, because most of the efforts to identify the behavior of liars and truth-tellers has highlighted nonverbal signals.

Miller and Stiff have done a superb job of critically reviewing the theoretical perspectives and research findings, but more important, this book makes the reader think hard about difficult issues. Few would argue, for example, that an effectively functioning society needs to be guided by a reverence for honesty in human interaction. Nevertheless, we also know that keeping secrets, concealing information, and even outright dishonesty may also make worthwhile contributions to a desirable social environment. Even President Lincoln, who is referred to as "Honest Abe," was reportedly admired for his ability to be devious: "Without his immense skills for hesitating, obfuscating, and compromising, Lincoln could not have been in a position to define the great moral issues of the war."[1] In my opinion, a book that asks us to consider this perplexing coexistence of two seemingly contrary forces like truth and deception performs a valuable service. It provides the adrenalin for energetically reexamining our ideas in an area where stagnant beliefs and pat answers are likely to be dysfunctional.

Even though *Deceptive Communication* treats a complex subject, it is clearly written. It weighs the value of past theories and research methods and sets an agenda for future work. It is a book of many faces. And they are all inviting.

—MARK L. KNAPP

NOTE

1. Garry Wills, "Dishonest Abe," *Time* (October 5, 1992), pp. 41-42.

Foreword

This is a volume with modest objectives. Some 15 years ago, the two of us, along with a number of colleagues at Michigan State University whose names will emerge as this book progresses, began a program of research dealing with deceptive communication. Specifically, the lion's share of our research dealt with factors influencing people's ability to detect truthful and deceptive messages, including the description of differences between both actual and perceived truthful and deceptive messages and several other factors such as the influences of probing questions by the intended deceivee and the relative impact of verbal and nonverbal message cues. Our first modest objective is to synthesize the results of these investigations and to attempt to pull them together and arrive at some tentative conclusions even though we quickly admit that the issues we discuss are far from exhausted, and that, in fact, in some instances it is difficult to draw a logical coherent picture of the overall outcomes.

Our second modest objective is to share with readers some of the conclusions and biases we have reached regarding certain theoretical and methodological issues associated with the study of deceptive communication. Although we lay no claim to a thorough understanding of these matters, our work over the past 1 1/2 decades has inevitably caused us to develop some theoretical and methodological biases. We offer these biases for our readers' consideration, fully recognizing that there are realistic and cogent options to several of the positions we advocate.

Given these modest objectives, we have chosen largely to ignore many other interesting problems pursued by students of deceptive communication. For example, Robert Feldman and his colleagues (e.g., Feldman, 1982) have conducted an ongoing research program examining the developmental aspects of deception as they emerge in the communication of young children. Although we allude to the pioneering research of Paul Ekman and his colleagues (e.g., Ekman, 1985; Ekman & Friesen, 1974), we scarcely touch upon the numerous contributions of this group in the areas of nonverbal and verbal clues to deception. Finally, although we do not agree with Bavelas and her associates regarding the most useful way of conceptualizing deceptive communication (Bavelas, Black, Chovil, & Mullett, 1990), we find much to admire in the work of this group on questions associated with the process of equivocation.

We deem it important to acknowledge these omissions of choice because our work has guided us toward an ever-increasing awareness of the centrality of deception to everyday human communication. Beginning with a restricted view of deception as a particular persuasive strategy, we quickly realized that the phenomenon of deception is much more pervasive and is relevant to any message exchanged by human beings. Indeed, as Mark L. Knapp put it in personal correspondence with us, deception is the other side of truth; any message has the potential to be deceptive depending upon the motives or intent of the communicator. It is thus crucial to realize that every topic touching on human communication inevitably involves the issue of truth versus deception, thereby underlining the fact that the study of deception spans the entire gamut of communicative problems and issues.

Numerous people have provided invaluable advice and assistance on this project. In addition to the usual good offices of Sage Publications, we have been particularly fortunate to have the services of Mark Knapp, an expert himself on issues of deceptive communication, as our consulting editor. He has not only aided with the typical questions regarding production, he has also offered many useful suggestions regarding substantive decisions and changes.

As mentioned earlier, a number of colleagues have been involved in the studies reported here. We will not single them out for thanks, but we trust they know how much we appreciate their collaboration. Moreover, the appearance of their names in the authorship listings will reveal who they are.

Speaking of authorship listings, the "first" author offers a word of gratitude to his coauthor. As most readers are aware, the norms of authorship typically dictate that authorship order should be determined by the relative contributions of the coauthors. Although our collaboration commenced with this assumption, subsequent events, including the uncertainties of illness, have led to marked changes in the initial divisions of labor. Through it all Jim has steadfastly refused to consider changing the authorship order. Since no reputable volume, especially one concerning deceptive communication, should be grounded in a lie, the "first" author explicitly underscores that the order of authorship represents an act of collegiality and personal affection, not a testimony to the varying degrees of intellectual contribution.

1

Deceptive Communication in Late 20th Century Society

The messages American society sends about deceptive communication are, like the messages of many other societies, equivocal, inconsistent, and sometimes themselves deceptive. Although probably more universally compelling a century ago, the "George Washington and the Cherry Tree" myth still conveys an appealing image to many of us: The vision of a person clinging bravely to the ideal of truth despite the dire consequences it may presage. Conversely, on some occasions, we disagree sharply on the moral culpability of certain prevaricators: Should the deceptive messages of North and Poindexter directed to Congressional members cause them to be labeled criminals, patriots, or perhaps even legal criminals *but* political patriots?

This ethical ambivalence about the place of deceptive messages in our society is hardly surprising. On the one hand, the unqualified injunction, "Thou shalt not lie!" packs a much more powerful ideological punch than a watered-down version counseling, "Thou shall not lie—except under circumstances A, B, C, etc." Indeed, one can only speculate about the subsequent motive power of the Ten Commandments had each moral caveat been followed by disclaimers listing the situations in which it did not apply. Moreover, as several writers (e.g., Bok, 1979; Knapp & Comadena, 1979) have underscored, the communicative commerce of society can only proceed in an orderly, humane way when communicators accept the existence of a general norm of truthfulness. Once the floodgates are opened and a wave of deceptive messages inundates the social marketplace, communicative and moral chaos are all but inevitable.

Notwithstanding the arguments for the absolute primacy of truthful discourse, however, only the most stubborn ethical absolutist would undertake to defend the proposition that it is *never* justifiable to communicate deceptively. Individuals who refuse to spare the culinary feelings of a gracious host or of a friend seeking support for his or her sartorial tastes are typically not seen as crusaders for truth but rather as social boors. It would be an extremely rare physician who never sought to mislead a patient in the interest of the latter's medical care and psychological well-being. And in the arena of international relations, deceit is often sanctioned as a vital element of the deceiving nation's self-interest. For example, during the weeks preceding the World War II D-Day landing at Omaha Beach, allied commanders floated numerous verbal and nonverbal messages aimed at convincing the Germans that the landing would occur elsewhere. We have encountered no political scientists, historians, or ethical theorists who have chastised the Allied Command for its deceit and have advocated instead that the command should have volunteered the actual location of the landing, or at least have maintained a circumspect silence. In short, even though many pay lip service to the ideal rule of absolute truth, few argue that there are no exceptions to it.

To what extent is deception evident in some of the various communicative settings of our society, and what are its acceptable limits in these settings? Lest we stand accused of deceptiveness ourselves, we hasten to add that this volume does not claim nor does it even seek to provide answers to these complex questions. Our more modest overriding goals are to describe some of our own research findings dealing with deceptive communication and to provide some suggestions for future research priorities in this problem area. Nevertheless, as a prelude to pursuing these aims, it seems useful to sample the deceptive flavor of contemporary American society if for no other reason than to provide readers with a taste of the problem's complexity.

DECEPTIVE COMMUNICATION IN POLITICAL AFFAIRS

One sanctioned deceptive message is perhaps best thought of as a political "white lie." The seeds for this duplicity arc sown when a high-ranking member of an administration resigns under a cloud created by the member's own questionable ethics or poor political judgment— two relatively recent examples being the resignations of Bert Lance during the Carter administration and James Watt during the Reagan presidency. It scarcely requires a political pundit to understand that such resignations are typically greeted with sighs of relief by other high-ranking members of the administration. Notwithstanding this fact, official public announcements of the resignation never reflect a tone of relief or a note of recrimination. Instead, the public is assured that the resignation was accepted with the utmost reluctance, that the resignee has performed long and distinguished service for the nation, and that members of the administration are at a momentary loss as to how they will be able to continue without the sage counsel of the resignee.

That such deceptive messages are not only anticipated but also generally sanctioned can be best understood by considering the rhetorical circumstances facing the announcement-maker—typically, for major resignations, the ranking member of the administration. By this time it is amply clear that the resignee has become a political liability and that his or her political demise has resulted largely from fuzzy thinking or moral indiscretion. To state this candidly when announcing the resignation would serve no ends other than to rub additional salt in the wounds of a loyal supporter and to admit the administration's fallibility. Reading between the lines, then, the resignation announcement can be interpreted as follows: "Well, old political ally, you really fouled up here, and I've no choice but to dump you. But since everyone already knows that you erred, since you've worked diligently and loyally for me, and since I don't want to admit my mistake, I'll try to paint your exodus as positively as possible." When viewed in this light, politically mandated resignation announcements have much in common with funeral orations; indeed, the resignation often symbolizes the political death of the resignee, and just as the eulogizer often marks the actual passing in deceptively overstated terms, the administrative representative frequently marks the political passing in similar deceptive fashion.

A second area of sanctioned political deception, alluded to earlier, springs from the largely unchallenged hegemony of concepts such as nationalism and sovereignty as guides for the conduct of international relations. The prevailing *realpolitik* analysis holds that it is justifiable for sovereign states to practice deceit if it is in their self-interest to do so. Thus, reports about beachhead locales or enemy body counts are not to be judged primarily by their veracity but rather by the extent to which they further the self-interests of the reporting government.

As the concluding clause of the preceding sentence suggests, there is no assurance that lying will necessarily promote national self-interest. This is particularly true if the deceptive message is botched in some way, or if later events unmask the deceit. As the end of President

Eisenhower's second term neared, the Soviet Union announced that it had downed a U-2 spy plane operating within Soviet air space. The United States promptly denied the presence of any reconnaissance missions within the Soviet Union's boundaries. Shortly after the denial, Soviet Premier Khrushchev triumphantly produced not only pictures of the downed aircraft but also its captured pilot, Francis Gary Powers. Rather than furthering its self-interest by deceptively extricating itself from spying charges, the United States both damaged its competence and trustworthiness in the eyes of other nations and poisoned the immediate atmosphere for mutually beneficial negotiations with the Soviet Union. Although the truth would not have enhanced America's international image, it would have spawned less damage than the administration's ill-conceived deceptive attempt.

In totalitarian societies, where means are clearly subordinate to ends, there are virtually no restrictions on deceptive communication: Any deceptive message deemed consistent with national self-interest is sanctioned. In democracies such as the United States things are not this simple, for the prevailing ideology holds that political actors must evince a concern for both political ends *and* the means used in their pursuit. Stated differently, some communicative strategies are suspect even if they achieve the desired ends because the strategies are at odds with democratic processes. Two obvious examples of such dubious strategies are deception and coercion. Thus, for instance, debate regarding the ethical propriety of Oliver North's and John Poindexter's false testimony to Congress can center on two different issues: (1) Do such instances of deceptive communication further U.S. self-interest or do they deal a blow to it by undermining national and international credibility (an ends issue, which presumes lying is acceptable as long as it actually furthers national self-interest)? (2) Even if lying can be demonstrated to enhance certain areas of national self-interest, should it be countenanced in a democratic society (a *means* issue, which suggests that lying is an inappropriate communicative strategy even if it sometimes furthers political ends)?

Finally, there is an area of political discourse that has traditionally cried out for the presumption of truth. Holders of public office should be candid in reporting their attitudes, beliefs, and probable courses of action to the citizenry, especially when their messages seek to marshal political support. "Read my lips! No new taxes!" is taken as a solemn promise to avoid fresh forays into taxpayers' pocketbooks. Indeed, as some political strategists understand, such commitments are often viewed as timelessly cast in stone, thus permitting attacks on the veracity of political figures who recant a position articulated months or even years earlier. Even the most skeptical observers of the political scene must surely grant a meaningful distinction between opportunistic deceit and clinging stubbornly to past policies clearly out of touch with present political realities.

Although we have found no systematic evidence bearing on the question, we sense that even in this last area of discourse, many citizens are becoming more permissive, or at least more fatalistically accepting, of deceptive tactics. Certainly cynicism about the veracity of politicians is a venerable characteristic of the American voter, but this cynicism has typically been coupled with belief in the moral culpability and responsibility of the offending party. During recent campaigns, many political commentators and voters alike seem to have become resigned to the fact that deceptive communication is merely part of the "getting elected" game. This tone of resignation surfaces in statements justifying deceit on grounds that "it was just something that was said during the campaign," the implication being that campaign pledges can be expected to become inoperative on inauguration day. To the extent that citizens accept a shift from a norm of honesty to a norm of deceit, traditional democratic values relating to the need for an informed populace and debate about the substance of issues will be seriously threatened. Indeed, some critics of the current political scene contend that increasing reliance on the 30-second television sound bite as the campaign staple virtually ensures heavier bombardments of deceptive messages, if for no other reason than the fact that such truncated communications are likely to deceive by virtue of omission of relevant information.

How can we best summarize this brief sketch of the ways deceptive communication enters into late 20th century American political life? Certainly Americans retain a hearty skepticism concerning the truthfulness of political messages; for example, Bok (1979) reports that a 1975-1976 study by Cambridge Survey Research found that 69% of the American public believed its political leaders had *lied consistently* over the previous decade (1965-1975). Despite this continuing skepticism, however, we sense heightened resignation to the fact that deception plays an integral role in the political process, a resignation that we fear may blunt or silence the moral outrage of many Americans. Finally, although there is consensus that much deceptive communication goes on in the halls of Congress and in city hall alike, it is not so easy to specify how untruthful messages can be ferreted out, for although everybody has a pet theory about how a liar can be spotted, findings regarding the utility of these theories are not comforting. We will have more to say about the problem of accurate deception detection, both in the political arena and in other domains, in succeeding chapters.

DECEPTIVE COMMUNICATION IN
DAILY TRADE AND COMMERCE

In Alfred Hitchcock's classic, *North by Northwest,* Cary Grant, who portrays a character employed in advertising and public relations, is asked about the lying occurring in his chosen profession. "There are no lies," Grant replies, "only strategic exaggerations."

Cynical as this response may seem, it captures one persistent attitude about the competitive marketplace, a dog-eat-dog arena where persons are expected to fend for themselves. The venerable phrase "Caveat emptor!" reminds us that buyers are to beware and suggests that unwariness is likely to result in dire yet arguably justifiable consequences. Indeed, some social critics and economic analysts contend that individuals who would not think of communicating deceptively in other contexts have no qualms about doing so when commerce is involved.

Examples of deceptive communication in the commercial domain are numerous; indeed, readers can probably supply many instances from their own experiences. Not too long ago in Michigan, a muckraking article in a large newspaper focused on the frequent practice of turning back odometers on used cars. So common was the practice that a few specialists in odometer adjustments actually circulated among numerous car dealerships plying their trade. Although the act of changing the mileage reading, while deceptive, would not itself constitute deceptive communication, any subsequent claims by sellers that the altered reading represented actual mileage would be duplicitous; for that matter, potential buyers who took the odometer numbers themselves to be true would be victims of a deceptive message. Because used-car sellers are one of the most common stereotypes employed by comedians and social critics who wish to comment on dishonest business practices, most potential used-car buyers probably do ask questions about mileage readings, thus opening the door to possible deceptive responses.

To grant this dog-eat-dog, everybody for themselves dimension of commercial ideology and practice does not imply that tolerance for deceptive communication is universally shared by members of our society. Within both the private and governmental sectors, individuals and groups seek to protect consumers from the deceptive wiles of advertisers and sellers. Well-known consumer advocate Ralph Nader is a tireless watchdog for the "little person," and government agencies such as the Federal Trade Commission monitor advertising messages with an eye and ear toward curtailing deceit. Indeed, American society harbors a somewhat schizophrenic attitude toward deceptive communication in the marketplace: On the one hand, there is admiration, albeit sometimes grudging, for individuals capable of weaving effective messages that sell products and services by stretching the truth; on the other, there is the realization that profits resting on a foundation of lies and half-truths are antithetical to an ethical, just society.

Given the economic stakes involved, it is hardly surprising that much legal attention has focused on the issue of when advertising and sales messages should be regarded as deceptive. Table 1.1 summarizes the different kinds of potentially deceptive implications found in advertising messages (Preston, 1989). The large number of possible lies and half-truths encompassed by the 15 implications testifies forcefully to the problems encountered when attempting to assess the veracity of product claims. Moreover, many of the implications underscore the subtlety of certain deceptive tactics. As a single example, consider the "more or less" tactic: the claim that a product contains more of a supposedly beneficial substance than does its competitors' or less of a supposedly harmful substance (the Significance Implication). Probably it is the case that most people are "programmed" to infer that if some product contains more of a good thing, it will provide greater relief or greater pleasure for its consumers. Conversely, less of a bad thing is likely to be automatically equated with lower product risk; for example, if "Simon Pure" cigarettes contain less tars and nicotine than competing brands, health risks associated with smoking "Simon Pures" should be reduced. Even if the claim regarding tars and nicotine is true (a question related to the Proof Implication found in Table 1.1.), there is, of course, no necessary implication that "Simon Pures" are less dangerous to smokers' health. The difference may be of no significance to health claims; that is, it may be of trivial magnitude, or even if substantial, it may still have no implication for health risks; to resort to a whimsical example, exposure to 5 versus 10 cyanide pellets is unlikely to influence the probability of a premature demise.

TABLE 1.1

Types of Potentially Deceptive Implications Found in Advertising Messages

1. The Proof Implication

   A test of the product is explicitly claimed to exist, and it is implied the test amounts to proof of the accompanying claim.

   Explicit references are made to surveys, and it is implied the results constitute proof.

   Indirect references made to tests imply the existence of such tests, which in turn implies that they prove the accompanying claim.

   Explicit product claims are made that imply the existence of the type of evidence or basis appropriate for proof.

2. The Demonstration Implication

   A type of proof implication where the implication occurs by explicit content consisting of demonstrations of product performance, rather than by reference to tests or surveys. (Note: Explicitly false demonstrations—e.g., claiming to demonstrate a shaving cream will shave sandpaper when what is used is actually loose grains of sand sprinkled on plexiglass—are not included in this type of implication, although of course they are deceptive and illegal.)

3. The Reasonable Basis Implication

   Affirmative representations of a product's future performance, benefits, safety, etc., implicitly represent that there is a reasonable and substantial foundation in fact for making the claim. (Note: This implication can sometimes be pursued more easily and/or effectively than a proof implication; e.g., when an advertiser expressly states that tests support the advertising claim, instead of challenging the truth of the representation itself it may be charged that the claim is deceptive because it is unsubstantiated.)

4. The No Qualification Implication

   Product claims are broadly stated with no qualification, not even an inconspicuous one. (Note: A major difference between this implication and a proof implication is that for the latter, the proof typically does not exist, while for the former, the claim may be true provided an appropriate qualification is appended.)

5. The Ineffective Qualification Implication

   Product message content contains a qualification, but it is so inconspicuously and/or ineffectively integrated into the message that it is likely to be unnoticed by consumers. The conveyed claim does not include the qualification.

6. The Uniqueness Implication

   Claims of certain product features are accompanied by the implication that only this product has these features; e.g., not only does a particular brand of shortening have many attractive features for frying chicken, no competing brands have these qualities.

7. The Halo Implication

   A true claim of product superiority in one way causes consumers to see superiority claimed in one or more additional ways. (Note: This implication has been particularly rife in advertisements for headache remedies, where true claims about the amount of pain-relieving ingredients in pills have led to the groundless implication that they are more effective than competitors in relieving pain.)

8. The Confusing Resemblance Implication

   Use of a specific word or phrase in a product claim that is similar to a more familiar, understandable work or phrase falsely implies the latter; e.g., reference to a "Cashmora" sweater implies the sweater is cashmere or labeling a product "Aspercreme" implies that it contains aspirin.

9. The Ordinary Meaning Implication

   Words or phrases with ordinary meanings are used in product claims and are mistakenly interpreted as implying their ordinary meaning; e.g., a breakfast juice's claim of more "food energy" does not imply more nutrients (ordinary meaning), but instead means nothing other than calories.

10. The Contrast Implication

    A product is contrasted to a competitor to show truthfully a certain difference, the implication being that additional contrasts are valid. (Note: The true difference typically has less value to consumers than the false difference(s) would have if true.)

11. The Endorsement Implication

    Advertising messages center on celebrities or ordinary consumers trumpeting their satisfaction with the product, the implication being that consumers generally will experience the same satisfactions.

12. The Expertise Implication

    Product endorsers' advertised expertise, conceded to be true, is falsely implied to be relevant to the accompanying claims; e.g., a racing driver's expertise does not extend to judging the relative merits of toy automobiles.

13. The Significance Implication

    A message states a true but insignificant fact with the accompanying unjustified implication that the fact should matter to the consumer; e.g., while it may be true that a cigarette is lower in tars and nicotine than competing brands, the difference may be so small as to have no significant effect on health risks.

14. Product-Specific Implications

    Numerous implications (hence, elimination of "The" in labeling the category) that foster unjustified beliefs about a particular type of product's advantage; e.g., medicines may truthfully claim that they relieve symptoms while falsely implying they cure the disease or condition.

15. The Puffery Implication

    Messages contain nonfactual opinion statements praising the product, but they imply that the claim is nothing but subjective opinion and thus no objective factual basis for the claim exists nor is one intended to be conveyed. (Note: As the wording of this implication implies, puffery is typically not deemed deceptive. Nevertheless, this position creates some interesting issues; e.g., why attribute deception for implying a product is best when it is not [the Uniqueness Implication] and not attribute deception for specifically stating it is best when it is not [the Puffery Implication?])

NOTE: This table is based on an extensive discussion of legal, psychological, and communicative issues surrounding these potentially deceptive advertising messages found in "The Federal Trade Commission's Identification of Implications as Constituting Deceptive Advertising," by I. L. Preston, 1989, *University of Cincinnati Law Review, 57,* pp. 1243-1310, and has been approved for publication by the author. Because extended analysis of these issues, particularly the legal ones, is beyond both the scope of this book and the expertise of its authors, readers are encouraged to avail themselves of Preston's thoughtful examination. Another useful source for exploring these issues is: *Deceptive Advertising: Behavioral Study of a Legal Concept* by J. I. Richards, 1990, Hillsdale, NJ: Lawrence Erlbaum, especially chapters 2 and 3.

In seeking to assess the relative veracity of advertising messages, the Federal Trade Commission faces a complex psychological, communicative, and legal task. For the most part, its decisions assume a reasonably rational, objective, critical consumer who is capable of bringing some cognitive know-how and affective balance to the judgmental task. Thus, puffery—nonfactual opinion statements about a product's merits that are represented as nothing more than subjective applause—is usually not deemed deceptive because consumers should be able to determine the lack of factual foundation for the product's claim. The special status accorded puffery has itself generated debate as to whether or not it should be considered deceptive and has opened the door for arguments about the appropriate legal definition of puffery. Richards (1990) contends that some claims deemed "puffs" in F. T. C. decisions should not be labeled as such; rather, puffery should be limited to

> (a) those claims that reasonable people do not believe to be statements of fact, and (b) which cannot be substantiated as a true product quality. If either the truth of the product attribute can be determined by the advertiser, or consumers believe it to be a statement of fact (i.e., they believe the claim is substantiated), it is not puffery. (p. 41)

Such definitional, factual, and value questions capture the complex flavor of disputes centering on the deceptiveness of advertising messages.

Although in some cases it may be reasonable to assume an objective target audience, people's needs and predilections often set them up to be duped by advertising and promotional messages. When P. T. Barnum observed, "There's a sucker born every minute," his observation was partially grounded on the awareness that people are sometimes ripe for deceptive plucking. Reasons for their gullibility range from greed or the desire to get something for practically nothing to heartfelt concern about some serious personal problem that defies solution.

A convincing, albeit somewhat amusing example of how greed makes people more vulnerable to deceit can be drawn from the experiences of the first author of this volume. As a result of an inveterate interest in thoroughbred horse racing, his name has been distributed on mailing lists to scores of persons intent on selling "foolproof" betting systems to greedy consumers. Although the mailed promotional messages for these systems vary widely in terms of stylistic and format quality, they all share the following three persuasive characteristics:

1. *All of the systems promise fabulous immediate profits.* Typical claims include "Win an average of $8,000 a month immediately!" "Seventy-five percent winning selections and 50% winning exactas, perfectas, and daily doubles at all forms of horse and dog racing," and "I fully expect you to make a return of AT LEAST 100%—if your wagers on the POP selections total $1,000–you will win $1,000 . . . wager $5,000—win $5,000! . . . and that's just the tip of the iceberg—compared to the REAL POTENTIAL PROFITS."

2. *All of the systems identify winning horses with practically no thought or effort.* The ease of the system is trumpeted by comments such as "No charts . . . No figures . . . No complicated math. Your picks become so obvious they will jump off the paper!" "You will go through an average race—spot the contenders . . . and make your selections—in about 5 minutes! No more long hours . . . no more burning the midnight oil," and "The 'Lock' does all the thinking for you, so you can relax. It takes only minutes for the 'Lock' to tell you which is the best horse."

3. *All of the systems can be purchased for ridiculously low prices given their purported returns.* Many of them sell for as little as $25.00 with prices seldom exceeding $100.00. In addition, all are accompanied by an ostensible money-back guarantee if the user is dissatisfied with the results.

Taken together these three characteristics should alert almost anyone that the messages are all but certainly deceptive. If a system actually could produce extravagant profits with little energy expenditure (or for that matter, yield large returns in exchange for some hard work), its discoverer would not be offering it for sale widely at cut-rate prices. Instead, he or she would hoard the information (wide dissemination could adversely affect the odds on winning horses), or share the system's secrets sparingly with a few big bettors in return for large cash rewards. Moreover, the only proof offered for the supposedly huge profits generated consists of testimonials by unknown bettors and charts of previous races where the winners paid generous prices and were said to have been selected by the system—but because the system is unknown, it is impossible to ascertain the truth of this claim; furthermore, by sorting through many previous races, one could probably find a few races to support any system, no matter how harebrained and farfetched. Although a refund is guaranteed, mailing addresses are typically post office boxes or "suites," suggesting that by the time a refund was requested, the purveyor of the system would be long gone. Finally, in an informal ongoing study by the first author, more than 50 purveyors of these systems have been contacted and assured that if they would provide the system free of initial costs, they would receive a percentage of one year's winnings that would amount to many times their charge for the system *assuming it was even close to being as effective as they claimed.* Not one of the sellers has elected to even reply to this offer.

Despite the overwhelming likelihood that the sales pitches for such betting systems are bald-faced lies, more than 100 mailings have been received by the first author in the past year. This fact suggests a profitable market for the product. If so, it can probably be explained by the unrealistic belief that the system will yield substantial monetary rewards, a belief triggered by the hope that it really is possible to get something for almost nothing. Indeed, a potentially truthful element of the testimonial letters mentioned earlier concerns their writers' stated unsuccessful attempts to strike it rich with many other systems, followed of course by praise for the discoverer of the system being hawked because it is the only one that "really works." In short, if people are strongly inclined to be deceived, even the most egregious lies will often be persuasive.

Given the selfish motives of the targets of this deceit, it may be difficult to feel much sympathy for them; their own avarice makes them willing victims of the liar. Others, however, are easily deceived for more justifiable reasons: It is neither surprising nor personally damaging to discover that individuals faced with serious health problems are highly susceptible to deceptive messages singing the praises of some new "miracle drug," or that persons shouldering serious economic burdens are deceived by promises of quick financial fixes. Desperate people are quick to seize at deceptive straws, and calculating liars know and shamelessly profit from this fact. Although the ideology and the pressures of the marketplace often discourage veracity, attempts to sustain a commercial truth ethic are in society's long-term best interests.

DECEPTIVE COMMUNICATION
IN PERSONAL RELATIONSHIPS

Notwithstanding the fact that all of us are partly political and economic animals, most of us conduct the majority of our communicative commerce in personal relationships. Such relationships run the gamut from casual acquaintances to close friends and romantic partners. Furthermore, they differ sharply in terms of their importance to us, and hence, the time and energy we devote to them. Finally, the nature and consequences of deceptive interaction vary from relatively harmless exchanges seeking to enliven, add interest, or inject humor into the relationship to destructive, ego-debilitating confrontations that threaten the relationship's very life.

As with the political and economic sectors, there is ambivalence and disagreement about the role of deceptive communication in personal relationships. Some persons advocate a view bordering on absolutism; that is, they contend that deceit has no place in personal relationships. Such a "telling it like it is" posture was central to the ideology of youthful social reformers during the late 1960s: These critics from the so-called counterculture cried out against the duplicity of American society and counseled its citizens to "be authentic" and to "let it all hang out." To misrepresent one's feelings or opinions to even the slightest extent was viewed as a personal weakness and a concession to the ruling "establishment."

Although many of the criticisms offered by the 1960s counterculture possessed considerable merit, their notion of absolute veracity is beset with serious problems. When practiced religiously, it largely ignores the feelings of others. A communicative exercise practiced by some during the period of the 1960s consisted of a kind of "consciousness raising" in which group members collaborated in itemizing one member of the group's annoying characteristics and habits so that he or she might "grow and develop as a person." Whether such uninhibited criticism contributes to personal growth is extremely problematic; indeed, it is likely that these flights of negative reinforcement were more frequently destructive than constructive. At the very least, the doctrine of absolute veracity can be questioned as an ethnocentric relational viewpoint lacking in its concern for social tact or rhetorical sensitivity.

As sometimes practiced, the ideal of absolute veracity itself provides a vehicle for introducing deception into social relationships. In the guise of being disclosive and authentic, the "whole truth" often becomes something more: Biographical descriptions and personal experiences are tailored to reflect favorably upon the person relating them or are used to curry relational favor or power. Miller and Steinberg (1975) label one particularly Machiavellian manifestation of this tendency *apparent self-disclosure*. By "disclosing" what is apparently personally private information but which is actually not, either because the "discloser" does not consider it private or because the "information" is an outright lie, the target of the "disclosure" is motivated by the norm of reciprocity (Gouldner, 1960) to provide genuinely private information about himself or herself. Because such information is an important source of relational power, the apparent self-discloser gains an advantage. Thus, what appears to be an act of honesty and trust is actually a deceptive message used to further selfish interests.

Even if the ethical desirability of absolute veracity were to be endorsed, its achievement is doubtless a practical impossibility. Some deceptive communication in personal relationships is a virtual certainty. The consequences of deceit vary, of course, both as a function of the content of the lie and the nature of the relationship. White lies told to spare the feelings of a relational partner or exaggerations inserted to spice up the interest or humor of an anecdote are less likely to detract from relational quality than falsehoods about monetary expenditures or relational transgressions; indeed, the former kinds of messages may actually contribute to relational enhancement. In casual acquaintanceships, potential dissemblers may be relatively unconcerned about the relational consequences of being caught in a lie; in close relationships, participants are typically quite concerned about the subsequent impact of detected deceit on the quality of the relationship (Miller, Mongeau, & Sleight, 1986).

Unpublished results of a survey by Miller, Mongeau, and Sleight (1984) underscore the ambivalence people experience regarding the role of deceptive communication in their close relationships. Cohabiting couples in a student housing area at Michigan State University were asked to complete independently identical questionnaires dealing with numerous aspects of the role of deceptive communication in close relationships. When asked to estimate how much deceptive communication occurs in close relationships *in general,* the predominant response was a modest amount. When asked how much deceptive communication occurred in *their own* relationships, however, almost all respondents replied hardly any. Interestingly, they also reported that while their partners practiced little or no deceit, they were confident that they could detect such communicative behavior should it rear its deceptive head. This strong truth bias coincides with findings by McCornack and Parks (1986) discussed more extensively in Chapter 6.

Some respondents were willing to grant the possibility of occasional flights of deceit by their partners. Most frequently, the content of the deceptive messages concerned annoying behaviors or habits not likely to be relationally threatening; for example, "He says he's quit smoking, but I know he keeps a pack at the office and sneaks a smoke now and then," and, "She says she's sticking by her diet, but I'm sure she has some candy squirreled away and that she pigs out on it when I'm not around." By contrast, not a single respondent expressed the belief that the partner had lied about relationally threatening issues such as romantic entanglements with third parties. Apparently and not surprisingly, some lies by relational intimates are normatively acceptable and conceivable but others are not. Of course, had Miller et al. (1984) been sampling responses from parties to troubled or endangered close relationships, a quite different deceptive picture might have been painted.

At the risk of redundancy, then, we repeat a shopworn conclusion: The question of the role of deceptive communication in social relationships is complex and does not admit to any simple, sovereign generalizations. Although some dissembling is permissible (and in certain cases, even desirable) there are limits to the amount and kinds of deceptive messages that will be tolerated. Particularly in close relationships, most individuals apparently subscribe to Bok's (1979, p. 263) conclusion that "Trust and integrity are precious resources, easily squandered, hard to regain. They can thrive only on a foundation of respect for veracity."

SUMMARY

We commenced this chapter with the goal of capturing a bit of the complexity surrounding the status of deception in contemporary society. Admittedly, we have not provided an extensive survey of the contexts within which deceptive communication can occur; other writers (e.g., Bok, 1979) delve into these settings much more thoroughly. Our brief journey into the deceptive aspects of politics, commerce, and social relationships should at least reveal the many definitional, factual, and value questions lurking there, and if nothing else, underscore the fact that the modest research programs discussed in subsequent chapters have but scratched the surface of the problem.

2

Conceptualizing and Defining Deceptive Communication

In Chapter 1, we used the term *deceptive communication* frequently without defining it. At first glance, the task of stipulating a definition for the term seems relatively simple, but as we will underscore in this chapter, numerous definitional problems quickly surface. Indeed, the term *deceptive communication* itself is aptly characterized as deceptively simple. As a beginning step in sorting out some of the important distinctions involved, consider the following three hypothetical scenarios:

Scenario 1: Greg arrives at his Monday morning communication class and takes his usual seat next to his friend Dani:

Dani: "Hi, Greg! What did you do this weekend?"

Greg: "Friday night I went to see *Cape Fear* at the Meridian Theatre; Saturday we played some basketball at the IM; Saturday night we went to the game, and Sunday I just hung around the dorm and studied for our midterm.

Dani: "Sounds like a pretty busy weekend."

Scenario 2: Greg and Dani, who are now dating steadily, are trying to decide on a video to rent for the evening:

Dani: "Did you ever see *When Harry Met Sally?*"

Greg: "Yeah, I saw it last year when I was home during Thanksgiving break. I thought it was a great movie!"

Dani: "You couldn't have seen it then because it wasn't released until December."

Greg: "Really? Then it must have been during Christmas break."

Dani: "That makes sense."

> Scenario 3: Greg has just arrived back at their apartment after a day in class and is immediately confronted by Dani:

Dani: "Remember when you were working on problems at the Computer Center last Wednesday night. I forgot to ask; did you get a lot of work done?"

Greg: "Yes, I finished all of my out-of-class problems for the next 2 weeks."

Dani: "That's real interesting that you could be so productive since Tricia Bender says she saw you drinking beer with a couple of girls and some guy at the Airliner!"

Greg: "Now just a minute . . ."

The first commonplace scenario illustrates that all communication, save for the shortest, rudimentary exchanges, is synoptic. Upon being asked for an account of their activities and behaviors, people invariably report only a small subset of the relevant information. Thus, during the weekend in question, Greg obviously did many other things than those activities he reports to Dani. Moreover, should a mutual acquaintance later query Dani about Greg's weekend activities, Dani probably will omit some of the information contained in Greg's original message, a truncative process illustrated informally by the common party game where a message originated by one individual changes sharply as it is passed on from one person to another and documented more formally by the *leveling* effect observed in studies of rumor transmission (e.g., Allport & Postman, 1945).

There are at least two reasons for the inherent synopticity of communicative exchanges. The first obvious reason concerns the limitations of human memory. Even if Greg consciously were to attempt to remember *everything* he experienced in 48 hours, he would find it impossible. As a consequence, he relates a few of the more salient, memorable moments of the weekend and omits innumerable less memorable happenings. What is remembered and forgotten depends in part on the priorities and needs of the communicator: If Greg is ardently involved with athletics, he will likely recall participating in or watching sporting events, but if the way to his heart is through his stomach, he will probably relate some of his more memorable eating experiences of the weekend.

A second, somewhat more subtle reason for omitting large chunks of information rests on a mutually understood rule underlying Dani's question. Both parties understand that her inquiry is not to be stretched to its literal extreme. She does not want to hear a laborious, event-by-event account of Greg's entire weekend doings, any more than someone who greet another with the query, "How are you doing?" expects a detailed report of the person's physical, economic, psychological, and social well-being. What is being requested is a glossed account of the weekend; indeed, such questions are often motivated by the desire to show interest and concern for the other, rather than any strong curiosity about the other's activities. Most of us have known individuals who always feel compelled to embark on a long, boring, monotonous monologue that attempts to capture every trivial detail of an event or anecdote, and such persons are not frequently sought out for conversations.

Whatever the precise reason, virtually all communicative exchanges are marked by the omission of information. Such inherent incompleteness renders possible the argument that all communication is, in a certain sense, deceptive. Although it might be philosophically or intellectually stimulating to advocate such a position—or just good, plain fun to engage in coffeeshop argument for this proposition—ordinary usage of the term *deceptive communication and its numerous synonyms assumes no such implication. Selectivity and oversimplification are usually not considered deceptive unless the message recipient has reason to suspect the message source of duplicity.* Indeed, given the absence of suspected deceit, communication probably occurs with little or no awareness of the truncated nature of the exchange. Thus, given the circumstances of Scenario 1, Dani is unlikely to recognize consciously that Greg omitted many of the particulars of his weekend.

Just as communicators may omit relevant information from their messages, they may also include factually inaccurate statements (Scenario 2). Greg mistakenly indicates that he saw a movie before it was released. Dani corrects him, and Greg admits his error immediately. Of course, Greg might not necessarily have surrendered this easily; we have all witnessed (and doubtless participated in) silly arguments about some factual question where all parties stubbornly clung to their positions. In such instances, the dispute is either left unresolved (with all disputants continuing to believe they are correct) or someone runs down evidence that demonstrates the correctness of her or his viewpoint.

No matter how the issue is resolved, the introduction of inaccurate information in such situations is not typically thought to be deceptive. "To affirm a falsehood when we are unaware that it is false is not a lie" (Eck, 1970, p. 25). Informational errors perceived as honest slipups are never equated with lying and deceit. Similarly, prior commitments and promises that must be recanted because of unanticipated intervening events are seldom deemed to be deceptive; only a small child would accuse his or her father of lying if a promised ski trip were to be postponed because the father subsequently broke his leg. In the language of communicator credibility (Berlo, Lemert, & Mertz, 1969, 1970; McCroskey, 1966) honest error relates to *competence* while deceptiveness relates to *trustworthiness*. Most of us are acquainted with persons who are frequently confused and mistaken about things, and although we may regard them as marginally competent or scatterbrained, we do not brand them liars.

As the dialogue suggests, the relational and communicative circumstances surrounding Scenario 3 vary markedly from those found in Scenarios 1 and 2. Her conversation with a third party has led Dani to believe that Greg misled her about his Wednesday evening activities. Rather than confronting him directly, Dani chooses to inquire in a way that requires Greg either to change his story or to stick with the studying story line. When he chooses the latter path, she immediately confronts him with the discrepancy between his reported actions and the actions ostensibly observed by Tricia, the third party.

Several comments are warranted by this dialogue. First, it should be emphasized that Greg may have committed no relational transgression. Tricia may have been honestly mistaken in her identification (similar to Greg's error in Scenario 2), or for some reason, she may even be dissembling (which Dani now suspects of Greg). Greg may have taken a break from studying to have a quick beer (the length of time Tricia saw him in the bar is unclear), or he could be having a hasty nightcap before returning to the apartment (the time of evening is also unclear). Thus, the dialogue may play itself out in numerous ways, depending upon how Greg responds to Dani's veiled attack on his honesty.

Of primary importance to the present discussion is the fact that Greg's message per se does not differ from his messages in Scenarios 1 and 2; all three scenarios are characterized by omitted and/or inaccurate information. *What does differ in Scenario 3 is Dani's perception of Greg's intent:* In the first two instances, she reveals no suspicion that Greg's omissions and inaccuracies are meant to deceive her, but in Scenario 3 she clearly expects a deceptive violation of relational rules and leaps on Greg's response quickly when it squares with her expectations. Thus, to be considered potentially deceptive, communicative exchanges must involve perceptions by one or more of the involved parties of *intent to deceive.* Moreover, our position leads to the following definition of deceptive communication: *"message distortion resulting from deliberate falsification or omission of information by a communicator with the intent of stimulating in another, or others, a belief that the communicator himself or herself does not believe"* (Miller, 1983, pp. 92-93, italics in original).

Most students of deception and lying agree that conscious, deliberate intent to deceive is an integral defining aspect of deceptive communication (e.g., Bok, 1979; Eck, 1970; Knapp & Comadena, 1979; Ludwig, 1965). To put it somewhat differently, Ekman (1985) argues persuasively that a liar can choose whether or not to lie and that recounters of paranoid delusions, pathological liars, and those who for whatever reason believe their own misinformation should not be considered liars. We subscribe to this position, even though we are aware that the determination of intent sometimes poses vexing problems; furthermore, our definition of deceptive communication exempts messages generated under conditions of paranoia, pathological falsehood, and misguided belief as possible instances of deceptive communication.

Despite widespread acceptance of the intent criterion, a few writers have argued against its inclusion as a defining characteristic of deceptive communication. For example, Bavelas et al. (1990) opt for a strictly discourse-centered definition, calling into question definitions that impose non-discourse-related factors, such as the intent of the communicator, as defining criteria:

> Serious definitional (and therefore measurement) problems arise because of efforts to align formal definitions of deception with intuitive conceptions of the moral issues involved. The focus in traditional treatments of lying and deception has been on the liar rather than the lie, that is, on the speaker rather than the discourse and on detecting and protecting ourselves from unwanted lies rather than on studying deception itself. Perhaps understandably, a strong moral tone underlies theory and research on deception, one that contrasts honesty with dishonesty and responsibility with reprehensibility, so that its theorists struggle to define lying in a way that includes "bad" lies and exculpates "good" lies. But it is this quasilegal approach that has made adequate scientific definition virtually impossible, as the primary, discourse-base definition (the veridicality of information in the message) is arbitrarily expanded or narrowed by noninformational criteria such as the motivation, justification, or effects of the message. (pp. 173-174)

Although agreeing with some of the points made by Bavelas et al., we shall explain briefly why we believe it is scientifically inadequate and socially dysfunctional to ground a definition of deceptive communication solely on the accuracy of information contained in the message.

As a beginning step, we disagree with Bavelas et al.'s judgment that inclusion of nondiscourse factors such as communicator intent in definitions of lying and deceptive communication signals an air of excessive moral preoccupation on the part of theorists and researchers. To be sure, in the world of daily communicative commerce, questions and accusations concerning liars and lying have strong moral overtones, and as we will suggest shortly, this fact constitutes one strong reason for invoking the notion of communicator intent when defining deceptive communication. Notwithstanding this fact, we believe that investigational priorities and justifiable theoretical and social considerations, not moral outrage, have led to the emphasis on communicator motivation and intent.

Most of the early concern with deceptive communication originated with persons sharing a keen interest in nonverbal communication (e.g., Ekman & Friesen, 1969, 1972, 1974; Feldman, Devin-Sheehan, & Allen, 1978; Hocking, Bauchner, Kaminski, & Miller, 1979; Knapp, Hart, & Dennis, 1974; Motley, 1974; Zuckerman, DeFrank, Hall, Larrance, & Rosenthal, 1979). Because most discussions of the importance of nonverbal communication emphasize its value in unmasking liars, it is not surprising that much prior research has centered on the process of deception detection. Furthermore, most theoretical interpretations of the utility of nonverbal cues in detecting deception underscore the importance of communicator arousal. An inverse relationship is generally posited between arousal and deceptive success: The higher the arousal the less the likelihood of deceptive success (Ekman, 1985; Miller, 1983). Arousal, in turn, is seen as resulting from *the communicator's perception of her or his intent to deceive* with its attendant awareness of the possibility of being discovered and of the ethical social sanctions against lying. Obviously, honest information mistakes and inadvertent omissions often are insufficient to trigger emotional arousal, the key factor being awareness of deceptive intent. Thus while we agree with Bavelas et al. (1990) that an inordinate amount of research energy probably has been directed at the role of nonverbal communication in detecting deception, we question their contention that this lopsided picture results from investigators' moral preoccupations.

In addition to pragmatic matters of research priorities, there are also sound theoretical and social reasons for making intent an essential ingredient of the definition of deceptive communication. As we indicated earlier, virtually all communicative exchanges are informationally non-veridical, either because of omissions or inaccuracies. Therefore, definitions focusing solely on the completeness and accuracy of messages render nearly all communication deceptive. Definitions that do little or nothing to refine or reduce the universe of a phenomenon strike us as sorely inadequate; indeed, if communication equals deceptive communication, the modifier is unnecessary. Moreover, if a definition results in the entire universe of discourse emerging as fair game for study, the claim that measurement problems are markedly alleviated gives rise to healthy skepticism.

Perhaps the most compelling reason for including the intent criterion in definitions of deceptive communication, however, is the fact that it is central to ordinary language users' meanings for the term. When "real world" communicators use words such as *lie, liar,* and *deceptive* they are not merely referring to the content of messages but also to the *motives* of communicators. Although we have no quarrel with some definitional tinkering and refining by theorists and researchers, we believe that when ordinary language concepts are employed, it is important to retain the gist of their conventional meanings. Research findings ideally should be generalizable to relevant everyday situations. Research that treats deceptive communication as *only* message inaccuracy does not comport with commonsense meanings and understandings of actual deceptive exchanges. A moment's reflection reveals that people respond to and deal very differently with those they perceive as purveyors of honest errors and those they pejoratively label as liars. Consequently, even if inclusion of the intent criterion poses additional definitional and measurement problems (and as noted above, we are unconvinced that it does), we prefer to cope with these problems rather than redefining the term *deceptive communication* in a way that is badly out of step with its ordinary meaning.

Clearly, additional conceptual distinctions could be made. For instance, since the term *lying* is ordinarily used to refer to the utterance of false statements, under certain circumstances it may be heuristic to reserve the label "lie" for messages relying on falsification of information to achieve the desired deceptive effects, and to conceive of deceptive communication as a more general category that also includes omission of information. Given such a perspective, all lies would be instances of deceptive communication, but not all instances of deceptive communication would involve lying. We shall refrain from further explorations of these conceptual nuances and turn to consideration of some ways of linking our conceptual definition of deceptive communication with observable communicative exchanges.

DEFINING DECEPTIVE COMMUNICATION OSTENSIVELY

Broadly speaking, people communicate deceptively about two informational domains: first, their own inner feelings; second, events, objects, or situations in the world external to them. As suggested in Chapter 1, many deceptive messages characterized as "white lies" concern the former domain. At the end of an exceedingly boring evening, someone may say that she or he had a "great time"; an unappetizing dinner may be described as a "delicious meal," or a sartorial nightmare may be verbally transformed to an "attractive coat." These kinds of self-feeling misrepresentations are typically considered harmless and may even be sanctioned as fulfilling norms of social acceptability and accountability. As Bok notes:

> In the eyes of many, such white lies do no harm, provide needed support and cheer, and help dispel gloom and boredom. They preserve the equilibrium and often the humaneness of social relationships, and are usually accepted as excusable so long as they do not become excessive. Many argue, moreover, that such deception is so helpful and at times so necessary that it must be tolerated as an exception to a general policy against lying. (1979, pp. 58-59)

Whether or not one accepts the view that "there are situations in which the intent to deceive becomes an almost compelling obligation" (Eck, 1970, p. 69), the fact remains that persons who insist on "telling their feelings like they are," no matter how hurtful their honesty may be to others, are socially frowned on by most minimally sensitive individuals.

Other feigned feeling displays stem from more questionable motives. Professions of love and concern for another when the communicator actually appears to harbor no such tender emotions and is merely maneuvering for financial or status advantage are likely to be viewed as Machiavellian manipulation. Ingratiation strategies (Jones, 1964; Jones & Wortman, 1972) such as insincere agreement or false flattery are typically viewed as morally suspect ways of currying favor with others.

And exaggerated or untrue assessments of others' capabilities and characters, as in the case of letters of recommendation, are often ethically questionable, particularly when it seems that the motive of the endorser is to foist an incompetent or immoral colleague onto someone else.

All of us have encountered self-feeling deceptions in our daily communicative activities. How can such deceptions be subjected to systematic investigations by students of deceptive communication? One commonly used approach is to involve research participants in situations that demand or at least strongly motivate deceptive messages. Thus, a number of studies (e.g., Brandt, Miller, & Hocking, 1980a, 1980b; deTurck & Miller, 1990; Hocking et al., 1979; Littlepage & Pineault, 1979; Miller, deTurck, & Kalbfleisch, 1983) have used a procedure modeled after one employed by Ekman and Friesen (1974), in which research participants report their emotional states while viewing pleasant and unpleasant slides. Specifically, Ekman and Friesen asked student nurses to view slides of both beautiful landscapes and badly injured burn victims. For each slide, the nurses were instructed to say they were feeling happy, contented, and relaxed; hence, they were instructed to tell the truth when viewing the pleasant slides and to lie when viewing the unpleasant ones. Nurses were told their responses would be viewed by others who would make judgments about the truthfulness of each message. They were also told it was important to do well on this "test" because nurses sometimes have to deceive patients about their health or their treatment. Finally, they were told their scores would be available for scrutiny by members of the nursing school faculty.

Note how these procedures capture the main features of our conceptual definition of deceptive communication. The nurses' responses to the unpleasant slides are distorted by falsification of information; that is, they indicate that they are feeling happy and relaxed while viewing the badly injured burn victims, when they are most likely feeling tense and unhappy (the qualifier "most likely" recognizes the remote possibility that a particularly sadistic person might not experience negative affect when viewing the burn victims, and therefore would not be lying, although on occasions when we have used the procedure we have yet to encounter anyone who was not disturbed by these graphic pictures). Furthermore, these distorted messages aimed at inducing the belief in subsequent observers that the nurses were happy and content when actually they were not, thus satisfying the intent criterion. In addition, the information about the importance of deceiving effectively and sharing their results with nursing faculty sought to heighten the salience and importance of the deceptive task, a move aimed at producing increased arousal.

A second procedure for generating truthful and deceptive messages about self-feelings has been used in several recent studies by Buller and his colleagues (Buller, Comstock, Aune, & Strzyzewski, 1989; Buller, Strzyzewski, & Comstock, 1991; Buller, Strzyzewski, & Hunsaker, 1991). This protocol requires research participants to respond either truthfully or untruthfully to items on a personality scale, the Crown and Marlowe Social Desirability Scale (Crown & Marlowe, 1964). Truth-tellers and liars are then placed in interview situations where they are questioned about their answers, and regardless of their veracity, all the respondents seek to convince their questioners that they have answered candidly.

This procedure also corresponds nicely with our conceptual definition of deceptive communication. One possible research limitation concerns the degree of relational familiarity existing between potential deceivers and detectors. For relative strangers, the content of the truthful and untruthful answers poses no problem, but if the communicators are well acquainted, the detector is likely to know that the deceiver's answers do not mirror her or his personality. As a consequence, accurate veracity judgments may be unrelated to factors associated with the communicative exchange, typically the area of investigatory interest, and may simply reflect the detector's knowledge that the professed personality characteristics are at odds with the defier's actual personality.

Turning to the second broad domain of deceptive messages, it is obvious that informational omissions and inaccuracies about events, objects, and situations in the external world are commonplace deceptive commerce. People lie about everything from the size of the fish they catch to the size of their annual income, the latter being subject to exaggeration in either direction depending upon whether the audience is an impressionable acquaintance or a representative of the Internal Revenue Service. Wayward students deny cheating and plagiarism; political leaders plead innocence of involvement in shady practices; and acquaintances recently returned from international travel begin a sentence with, "When I was in Paris . . . ," conveniently forgetting to add that their Paris adventures were limited to a brief refueling stop at the airport. Every day, controversies arise where it is apparent that one of the parties is dissembling about matters of fact, as in the case of the markedly discrepant accounts provided by the accusers and the accused in criminal trials such as rape. Although the consequences of these distorted messages range from harmless to heinous, there is no question about the frequent incidence of such deceptive communication.

Previous studies have relied on various approaches to induce persons to lie about external matters of fact. One of the most frequently used procedures, developed by Exline and his colleagues (1970) and hereafter referred to as the *Exline procedure,* involves implicating persons in a cheating incident (see, e.g., Bauchner, Brandt, & Miller, 1977; Bauchner, Kaplan, & Miller, 1980; deTurck & Miller, 1985; Exline, Thibaut, Hickey, & Gumpert, 1970; Shulman, 1973; Stiff & Miller, 1986). Research participants are told they will be working at a perceptual task with another person, supposedly a naive participant like themselves but actually a confederate of the researcher. The ambiguous task requires that they cooperatively reach an estimate of the number of dots on a series of 4 by 6 inch note cards. In most studies using the Exline procedure, the teams are also told that the dyad who scores highest on the task will receive a monetary reward.

After several estimation trials, the experimenter leaves the room on some pretext such as "taking an important phone call from the senior investigator on the project." Upon being summoned, the experimenter announces he or she will return shortly, suggests the two members of the dyad discuss their strategy for arriving at estimates, and departs, leaving a manila folder on a chair. At this point, the cheating manipulation occurs: If the research participant has been randomly assigned to a truthful condition, the confederate initiates a general discussion about strategic alternatives (because of the ambiguity of the task, alternatives are typically not very specific or helpful); if the participant has been assigned to a deceptive condition, the confederate points out the folder, opines that the answers for the remaining trials are probably in it, and advocates obtaining them so they dyad can "do well and win the monetary award." Regardless of the naive participant's response to this cheating suggestion, the confederate obtains the folder, points out the answers to the participant, and proceeds to memorize them.

At this point, the experimenter returns to the room and the remaining estimation trials are conducted. In the truthful condition, dyad members arrive at estimates using whatever strategy they can devise, but in the deceptive condition, they almost invariably report estimates closely approximating the ones memorized during the experimenter's absence. When the trials are completed and the scores ostensibly calculated, the experimenter tells all dyads in both conditions that they have performed better than any other dyad, and that they have done particularly well in the trials occurring after the experimenter's absence. Because of the ambiguity of the task, naive participants are easily convinced of their dyad's effectiveness in the perceptual task.

To generate truthful and deceptive messages, the experimenter next requests that the dyad members answer some interview questions about their strategies for solving the task, "because you have done so much better than any other group." To continue to mask the fact that one dyad member is a confederate, the experimenter targets the naive participant for the first interview, indicating that the confederate will be interviewed next.

During the interviews that follow, participants in the truthful condition may have difficulty articulating specific performance-enhancing strategies, but they will not be under pressure to prevaricate. Conversely, participants in the deceptive condition, who believe their success resulted from cheating, have the choice of admitting their guilt, thereby reflecting unfavorably on their own honesty and also forfeiting the monetary reward due to both their partners and themselves, or conjuring up deceptive messages invoking nonexistent strategies. Because participants seldom confess to cheating, the interviews typically generate deceptive messages for present or future judgment by detectors.

We have described the Exline procedure in detail because of its frequent use and because we believe it is a relatively involving procedure that produces heightened deceiver arousal. Consistent with the previously described approaches for inducing deceptive self-feeling messages, it closely conforms with the major elements of our conceptual definition of deceptive communication. Two limitations of the procedure should be noted: First, unlike the approaches described for generating self-feeling messages, the Exline procedure does not permit researchers to obtain both truthful and deceptive messages from the same communicator; either a participant is or is not implicated in cheating. Second, the details of the procedure themselves involve considerable deceptive communication by the researcher. We realize this may be troublesome to readers, and we will consider the issue more fully in later remarks concerning the ethics of research on deceptive communicators.

This section has not sought to provide an exhaustive, detailed description of all possible ways of generating deceptive messages; rather, we have tired to illustrate how the major elements of our conceptual definition can be translated into empirical procedures for studying deceptive transactions. Chapter 3 elaborates on the problems and limitations of these and other procedures, as do other portions of this book. Finally, we grant that none of the approaches described above involves studying deceptive communication in natural settings, but focus instead on procedures for generating messages in laboratory situations. One reason so little research has occurred in the former arena is because of the obvious difficulties in ascertaining whether naturally occurring messages meet the criteria of deceptiveness. Despite this thorny problem, we regret the paucity of natural-setting research and will have more to say about it later.

CONCEPTUALIZING DECEPTIVE COMMUNICATION AS PERSUASION

Throughout the first two chapters, we have mentioned numerous examples of deceptive communication ranging from relatively harmless to exceedingly manipulative and self-serving. No matter what their consequences, however, all of the deceptive messages alluded to share the common feature of seeking to affect someone else's beliefs, attitudes, and/or behaviors. *"Deceptive communication strives for persuasive ends; or, stated more precisely, deceptive communication is a general persuasive strategy that aims at influencing the beliefs, attitudes, and behaviors of others by means of deliberate message distortion"* (Miller, 1983, p. 99, italics in original). Thus, successful deception is seldom, if ever, the *end* sought by communicators, but is rather a *means* toward another persuasive goal. Returning to the earlier potentially deceptive scenario involving Greg and Dani, if Greg is being deceptive about his activities of Wednesday evening, his primary objective is not to convince Dani that he spent his time working on class problems at the computer center even though her acceptance of this mendacious assertion is crucial to his persuasive success. What Greg wishes to accomplish, by dispelling Dani's belief that he was actually at a bar drinking with mixed company, is avoidance of punishment by Dani as well as maintenance of Dani's positive attitudes about their romantic relationship. Truthful and untruthful information serves the same persuasive function, that is, both constitute warrants and evidence for explicit or implied claims offered by communicators.

Table 2.1 lists six typical deceptive communication situations and underscores the means-ends relationship between deceptive strategies and persuasive goals. In some, the persuasive goal rests on achieving a tangible personal reward (e.g., earning a sales commission) or avoiding

TABLE 2.1
Six Typical Deceptive Communication Situations and Their Persuasive Goals

Situation	Deceptive Aim	Persuasive Goal
A car salesman tells a potential buyer the mileage on the speedometer is accurate, when in fact he knows the mileage has been moved back.	To induce the potential buyer to believe that the mileage showing on the speedometer is accurate.	To get the potential buyer to pay "top dollar" for the car, thus ensuring a substantial commission for the salesman.
A son tells his parents he does not know how a window got broken, when in fact he broke it.	To induce the parents to believe that the son is innocent of any wrongdoing in the case of the broken window.	To avoid sanctions or punishment, and to maintain a positive self-image in his parent's eyes.
A senator tells his/her constituents that he/she did not accept a bribe, when in fact the senator did.	To induce the constituents to believe that no bribe was accepted.	To avoid being perceived as corrupt and dishonest, and also to maximize chances of a continued successful political career.
A pharmaceutical firm sings the benefits of a new drug, while at the same time failing to mention evidence that the drug has harmful side effects.	To induce prospective users to believe that the drug is medically beneficial and safe.	To promote sales of the drug, and also to protect the firm's scientific and commercial credibility.
A scientist reports important findings, when in fact the data for the research are falsified.	To induce other scientists to accept the authenticity of the falsified data.	To impress other scientists with the scientist's acumen, thereby enhancing his/her professional career.
A woman tells a friend she likes a new painting the friend has purchased, when in fact she finds it aesthetically displeasing.	To induce the friend to believe that the woman likes the painting when in fact she does not.	To reinforce positively the friend's perception that their aesthetic tastes coincide, and to maintain the positive tone of their relationship.

SOURCE: From "Telling It Like It Isn't and Not Telling It Like It Is: Some Thoughts on Deceptive Communication" (pp. 91–116) by G. R. Miller, in *The Jensen Lectures: Contemporary Communication Studies*, edited by J. I. Sisco, 1983. Tampa: University of South Florida. Used by permission.

a tangible punishment (e.g., being perceived as a corrupt, dishonest politician); in others, the goal is more relationally oriented (e.g., maintaining the positive tone of a friendly relationship); and in still others, both personal and relational goals are relevant (e.g., escaping punishment for breaking a window and maintaining a favorable parental relationship). In none of the situations is successful deceit the primary objective; rather, deceit furthers other persuasive goals. Indeed, it is difficult to imagine situations where mere success at dissembling is paramount. Ekman discusses the phenomenon of *duping delight,* where

> The lie may be viewed as an accomplishment, which feels good. The liar may feel excitement, either when anticipating the challenge or during the very moment of lying, when success is not yet certain. Afterward, there may be the pleasure that comes with relief, pride in the achievement, or feelings of smug contempt toward the target. (1985, p. 76)

At first glance, it may appear that the success of the lie itself is the persuasive goal, but actually, as Ekman reveals in the preceding comments, the end sought is some form of self-reinforcement or personal aggrandizement on the prevaricator's part. Even such an apparently benign deceit as misleading a gullible friend "may in large part be directed to others who are appreciating how well the gullible person is being taken in" (Ekman, 1985, p. 76).

Figure 2.1, which depicts the essential elements of a deceptive communication transaction, further demonstrates the utility of conceptualizing deceptive communication as a persuasive endeavor. All deceptive exchanges occur within particular social contexts, and in turn, these contexts are important determinants of both the strength of motivation to deceive and the probable deceptive success. Deceivers and intended deceivees respectively are affected by their relative motivation to deceive and to detect deception, which in turn is yoked with the consequences resulting from successful or unsuccessful performance of these two competing communicative roles. Finally, because the primary behavioral activities consist of the verbal and nonverbal components of the deceptive message, the deceiver attempts to control these behaviors so as to escape detection, while the intended deceivee searches for cues thought to signal deceptive intent.

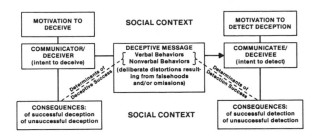

Figure 2.1. The Essential Elements of a Deceptive Communication Transaction

SOURCE: From "Telling It Like It Isn't and Not Telling It Like It Is: Some Thoughts on Deceptive Communication," by G. R. Miller, pp. 91-116 in *The Jensen Lectures: Contemporary Communication Studies,* edited by J. I. Sisco, 1983, Tampa: University of South Florida. Used by permission.

SUMMARY

Our aim in this chapter has been to stipulate a useful definition for the term *deceptive communication,* as well as to consider some of the crucial issues and distinctions associated with this conceptualizing and defining process. After explicating our definition, we described several available procedures for linking the definition to systematic observations. Finally, we argued that deceptive communication is best conceptualized as a general persuasive strategy, an argument that reinforces the status of deceptive communication as a theoretical construct in addition to its obvious pragmatic and social importance.

3

Investigating Deceptive Communication

Social scientists constantly strive to make objective observations of phenomena they study. Identification of phenomena is often relatively easy; the more difficult chore is to prevent biases and predilections from influencing the observations. However, unlike many communicative phenomena, deceptive transactions are as difficult to identify as they are to investigate. Because a communicator's intent to mislead is central to our definition of deception (see Chapter 2), it is extremely difficult to observe deceptive transactions as they naturally occur. Consider former President Reagan's denial of knowledge about the illegal shipment of U.S. funds to the Contras in Nicaragua. Though most of us have made judgments about his honesty in this instance, we may never be sure if the former President was truly uninformed or whether he intended to deceive the American public.

Because deception is difficult to recognize, researchers have relied on a variety of experimental and nonexperimental procedures to make observations and draw conclusions about deceptive transactions. In this chapter we discuss important characteristics of deceptive transactions and identify criteria for assessing the quality of observations made. We then describe several procedures used in prior research and evaluate them vis-à-vis the established criteria.

LABORATORY AND FIELD OBSERVATIONS

For many reasons it is often impractical to study deceptive communication in field settings. In addition to the problem of recognizing deception, ethical considerations limit the range of everyday deceptive transactions that are amenable to scientific observation. For example, deception between relational partners is probably a common occurrence, but it is difficult to observe without violating people's privacy. Such concerns limit the number of investigations situated in field settings.

More frequently, researchers employ laboratory settings that permit the structuring of interactions to isolate specific variables of interest and to control extraneous factors. The trade-off here is that experimental control often leads to questions about the generalizability of research findings. Indeed, we often encounter arguments suggesting that laboratory settings produce findings that have limited application in the "real world."

Such arguments falsely assume that research settings determine the generalizability of a study's findings. In fact, the research setting has little influence on a study's external validity. More important are the specific procedures used to make observations. If flawed observational procedures are employed, a study's conclusions will not be valid, regardless of the setting in which the observations were made. On the other hand, it has been our experience that both laboratory and field settings do produce valid and generalizable conclusions as long as proper procedures are adopted. Thus, we endorse Locke's position that, "what is needed when trying to determine the legitimacy of generalization is the identification of the essential features of field settings that need to be replicated in the lab" (1986, p. 7). In this chapter we will identify the *essential features* of natural deception transactions. We will use these features as the criteria to evaluate the validity of eight procedures frequently used in deception research.

ESSENTIAL FEATURES OF DECEPTIVE TRANSACTIONS

Because deception varies from situation to situation, features central to one deceptive interaction may be irrelevant to another. For example, the consequences of deception for a witness committing perjury are considerably greater than for people telling white lies in casual conversation. Thus, while many essential features are common across deceptive situations, not all of these characteristics are essential in every situation. The primary task for deception researchers is to design study procedures that replicate the essential features of deceptive situations in which the findings will be applied. Below we discuss several essential characteristics that are typical of deceptive transactions and provide the basis for evaluating the validity of study procedures.

Motivation to Deceive

The first essential characteristic is the communicator's *motivation to deceive* effectively. The *principle of veracity* holds that, in the absence of special circumstances, truthful statements are preferable to lies (Bok, 1979). As such, a decision to deceive is often accompanied by considerable motivation to do so effectively. Deceivers usually understand and weigh consequences associated with detection.

Often, the negative consequences of being caught in deception far outweigh the consequences of being truthful. For example, a child who lies about breaking a neighbor's window may face more severe punishment for lying than for having broken the window. In other situations, deceivers are motivated by the possibility of attaining positive outcomes that are less likely if the truth is told. For example, job applicants may exaggerate their expertise during an interview to increase their chances of gaining employment. The greater the consequences, the greater the motivation to deceive effectively. Though not all deceptive situations are of equal consequence, the validity of any deception study depends on the extent to which the motivation to deceive successfully matches the motivation of deceivers in situations in which the findings will be applied. This is particularly important in light of the effects of motivation on arousal and the production of nonverbal behaviors associated with deception (see Chapter 4).

Motivation to Detect Deception

Situations also vary in the extent to which targets of deceptive messages are motivated to detect the deception. For example, jurors are often required to sift through conflicting testimony before rendering a decision. In such cases, careful scrutiny of testimony is an indication of heightened motivation to detect deception. On the other hand, we can think of many situations in which targets lack motivation to detect deception. Consider a spouse who suspects his or her partner of relational transgressions, but lacks sufficient motivation to detect the deception. Sometimes people prefer "not to know" because they fear the relational, emotional, or economic consequences of detection. On the other hand, people may lack motivation simply because a situation is unimportant. In social settings, for example, phatic compliments are so pro forma and commonplace that few people ever worry about their veracity.

Just as there are consequences for deceivers who are detected, consequences exist for detectors who make accusations about another's veracity. These consequences are an important contributor to an individual's motivation to detect deception. As we argued above, in order to ensure the generalizability of study findings, researchers must consider detection motivation as a second "essential feature" of natural deceptive transactions.

Anticipation of Deception

Although deceptive transactions occur with some frequency, the vast majority of our everyday communication is truthful. Because most communicative experiences are truthful ones, people develop a truth bias—a generalized belief that our communicative partners are truthful. While people differ in this truth bias, most exhibit a high level of trust in others (McCornack & Levine, 1990), and this truth bias guides communicative transactions (McCornack & Parks, 1986; Stiff, Kim, & Ramesh, 1992). That is, in most communicative settings, people are unlikely to anticipate deception because they trust their partner is communicating honestly. Clearly, situations exist in which we anticipate deception. That we have come to expect deception from people in certain professions (politics and sales), however, does not negate the point that in many interactions we anticipate honesty.

Unfortunately, most laboratory investigations of deception detection cause participants to "set aside" their truth biases and heighten their anticipation of deception. While some experimental procedures instruct participants to expect deception, others more subtly ask participants to judge the character or trustworthiness of a source. Indeed, simply participating in an experimental study may be sufficient to artificially raise awareness and involvement with the interaction.

Because aroused suspicion and truth biases influence the process of deception detection (McCornack & Parks, 1986; Stiff et al., 1992), the generalizability of experimental studies of this process depends on the extent to which participants are heightened to suspect deception. Study procedures that cause participants to anticipate deception may produce findings that are generalizable only to those situations in which people anticipate or expect deception. It is essential that the anticipated level of deception created by experimental procedures "matches" the level found in communicative settings to which the findings are applied.

Sanctioned Deception

In most communicative transactions, participants decide for themselves whether to deceive or tell the truth. Even in situations where people attempt to shift the responsibility for deception to some higher authority, deceivers still perceive that they may be held personally accountable for their decision. For example, Oliver North contended in his trial following the Iran-*Contra* Investigation that his superiors knew he lied to Congress and that he believed it was his duty to do so. Though he used the defense of sanctioned deception, he no doubt realized that others would attempt to hold him accountable for his actions if the deception was detected.

While the lion's share of natural deceptive transactions involve deceivers who may be held accountable for avoiding the truth, many procedures for studying deception absolve participants of the responsibilities associated with deceptive attempts. In most laboratory studies, the decision to deceive is made by an experimenter who requests research participants to communicate truthfully or deceptively. When such requests are made, responsibility for the deception shifts from the communicator to the experimenter. In essence, deception is sanctioned by the experimenter and carried out by participants who are primarily concerned with fulfilling the role of "good subject."

Because deception is often unsanctioned in natural transactions, the motives of participants who deceive simply to carry out an experimenter's instructions to deceive must be scrutinized. To the extent that these intentions and motives differ from those in natural transactions, results from studies involving sanctioned deception may lack generalizability. In this regard, unsanctioned deception serves as a third essential element of naturally occurring deceptive transactions.

Relational Development

One factor thought to influence the deception process is the extent to which interactants are familiar with one another. Miller and Steinberg (1975) argue that as relationships become more developed, participants gain person-specific information about one another. This information is used to make predictions about a partner's reactions to particular communicative messages. Applied in deceptive contexts, such knowledge allows one to tailor deceptive messages to match another's expectations and hence avoid detection. Though this issue has not been widely studied, relational knowledge may exert considerable influence on the production of deceptive messages.

Knowledge about others is also likely to affect deception detection. People in well-developed relationships have the opportunity to identify deviations from their partners' communicative styles when making judgments of veracity. For example, one may recognize that a usually talkative partner avoids superfluous conversation during deception. However, strangers lacking knowledge about this person's typical communicative style are less likely to recognize the change in verbosity signaling deception. On the other hand, as we suggested earlier in this chapter, people in well-developed relationships may have a vested interest in *not* detecting a partner's deception.

Though the effects of relational knowledge are probably complex, these examples illustrate the importance of relational development on the deception process. Because deception among relational intimates is a very private form of communication, most researchers have avoided the ethical constraints of such studies by focusing exclusively on deception between strangers. As such, the findings of many prior studies may have limited application for deception in a wide variety of interpersonal relationships.

CRITERIA FOR EVALUATING RESEARCH PROCEDURES

The essential features of motivation to deceive and detect deception, anticipation of deceit, unsanctioned deceptive behavior, and relational development provide the foundation for assessing the generalizability of deception research. However, our evaluation of research procedures extends beyond assessments of external validity. We believe it is appropriate to apply nine criteria to determine the merits of deception research procedures:

1. Are participants sufficiently motivated to deceive?
2. Are participants sufficiently motivated to detect deception?
3. Are participants likely to anticipate deception?
4. Is the deception sanctioned by the experimenter?
5. Is the procedure appropriate for investigating relational deception?
6. Can verbal and nonverbal correlates of deception be investigated?
7. Can deception detection be investigated?
8. Does the procedure conceptualize deception as a transactive process?
9. Will this procedure raise concerns about ethical use of human research participants?

The first four questions concern the potential generalizability of research findings. Affirmative answers to Questions 1 and 2, combined with negative answers to questions 3 and 4, provide the foundation for generalizing study findings to natural deceptive situations. Questions 5, 6, and 7 identify the range of conceptual questions that can be answered with a given procedure. Affirmative answers to these three questions indicate that the procedure is flexible enough to address a wide variety of issues.

Question 8 focuses on the extent to which the research design conforms with current conceptualizations of communication. Though most scholars define communication as a transactional process, few research procedures study communication transactionally. This is particularly true of deception research. For example, many deception detection studies expose people to a single uninterrupted message and ask them to judge the source's veracity. Such procedures fail to consider the importance of a message recipient's reactions to the source on subsequent statements produced by the source. An affirmative response to Question 8 suggests that the procedure considers the simultaneous influences of sources and targets on the deception process.

Question 9 concerns the extent to which the procedure meets ethical guidelines for use of human research participants. Though these guidelines vary across universities, there is considerable consensus on several issues. First, participants must be made fully aware of the requirements of their participation before the study begins. Second, participation must be voluntary, affording participants the opportunity to quit at any time during the investigation. Third, precautions must be taken to ensure participants do not suffer harmful physical or psychological consequences as a result of participating in the study. Fourth, the study must be completely explained to participants following their participation. This debriefing procedure should include an offer to make the results of the study available to interested participants.

Procedures that raise ethical concerns are not necessarily unethical for use. Quite often these concerns can be addressed with additional precautions and more complete debriefing procedures. We will revisit this general issue in Chapter 7 when we discuss the ethical implications of investigating deceptive communication. Nevertheless, ethical considerations are central to evaluating the utility of research procedures, and we will briefly address them as we proceed with our discussion of various research procedures.

EVALUATING PROCEDURES FOR STUDYING DECEPTION

Our conception of an "ideal research paradigm" is one that meets the requirements suggested by each of the above criteria (Table 3.1). Thus, an ideal procedure would be one in which there is sufficient motivation to deceive and to detect deception, anticipation of deception is not heightened by researchers, deception is not sanctioned by researchers, relational deception can be investigated, judgments of detection accuracy can be investigated, deception is conceptualized as a transactive process, and there are no concerns about the ethical use of human research participants. While few procedures are likely to meet all of these criteria, characteristics of an ideal research procedure provide one basis for evaluating procedures frequently employed in deception research.

In this section we use these criteria to evaluate the utility of seven procedures for observing deceptive transactions. These evaluations are based on descriptions of standard procedures. Modification of these "generic" procedures is common as researchers "tailor" them to study a variety of issues. Such modifications may be sufficient to alter our overall assessment of the utility of a general procedure. Our intent is not to evaluate every prior study, but rather to compare the utility of various methods of inquiry.

Uninterrupted Message Presentations

One of the first deception studies in the field of communication (Knapp et al., 1974) used a procedure we label the *uninterrupted message presentation* procedure. Variations of this procedure have been very popular among researchers because it is easy to use and because the Knapp et al. study provided a model for those that followed.

Knapp et al. (1974) asked military veterans to present a message that accurately represented their views about increasing educational benefits for veterans (truthful message condition) and a message reflecting a position they did not endorse (deceptive message condition). Though interviewers were used to elicit respondents' positions on the issue, they did not interrupt or question the validity of participants' responses, and interview questions were held constant across interviews.

The Knapp et al. procedure is representative of studies of this genre. Other investigations using this general procedure asked respondents to lie or to tell the truth about where they traveled during a recent vacation (Cody, Marston, & Foster, 1984), or about personal and demographic

TABLE 3.1
Characteristics of Deception Research Procedures

Research Procedure / Ideal Research Procedure	Procedure Characteristic								
	1	2	3	4	5	6	7	8	9
Ideal Research Procedure	Yes	Yes	No	No	Yes	Yes	Yes	Yes	No
Uninterrupted Message Presentations	No	No	Yes	Yes	No	Yes	Yes	No	No
Reaction Assessments	Yes	No	Yes	Yes	No	Yes	Yes	No	No
Exline Procedure	Yes	No	Yes	No	No	Yes	Yes	No	Yes
Relational Interviews	?	?	Yes	Yes	Yes	Yes	Yes	Yes	No
Simulated Interviews	N/A	No	Yes	N/A	No	No	Yes	No	No
Survey Interviews	Yes	Yes	No	No	Yes	?	Yes	?	No
Interaction Analysis	Yes	Yes	?	No	No	Yes	Yes	Yes	No

Description of Study Characteristics

1. Are participants sufficiently motivated to deceive?
2. Are participants sufficiently motivated to detect deception?
3. Are participants likely to anticipate deception?
4. Is the deception sanctioned?
5. Is the procedure appropriate for investigating relational deception?
6. Can verbal *and* nonverbal correlates of deception be investigated?
7. Can judgments of deception and/or detection accuracy be investigated?
8. Does the procedure conceptualize deception as a transactive process?
9. Will this procedure raise concerns about ethical use of human research participants?

information (Cody & O'Hair, 1983). Essentially, this procedure asks respondents to lie or communicate truthfully while presenting a single, uninterrupted message. Videotaped records of these presentations permit researchers to investigate the verbal and nonverbal cues associated with truthful and deceptive messages. In addition, researchers have the option of showing these videotapes to a second group of participants charged with the task of judging the veracity of each message presentation. Thus this procedure is useful for answering questions about both deception and deception detection (Table 3.1).

Two major limitations of this procedure stem from its unidirectional approach to studying deceptive transactions. Because interview protocols in these studies are structured, questions asked by interviewers do not vary across interviews. As such, this procedure overlooks the importance of a target's questions on the deception process and adopts a linear approach to communication that does not fully represent deceptive transactions in natural contexts.

This procedure also suffers from an inability to motivate people to deceive or detect deception effectively. Though some researchers using this procedure have offered monetary rewards (or extra course credit) for both effective deception and accurate detection, the levels of motivation experienced by participants in such studies remain relatively low. Thus, investigations using this procedure may lack generalizability to a wide range of naturally occurring deceptive transactions in which people are highly motivated to deceive and/or detect deception. In addition participants charged with the task of detecting deception are typically informed that a portion of the sources communicated truthfully while others were deceptive. As a result, detectors in studies using this procedure may have unrealistically high expectations of deception.

Perhaps the most significant limitation of the uninterrupted message presentation procedure is that the deception is typically sanctioned, removing the responsibility for veracity from deceivers. As mentioned previously, sanctioning deception is likely to have significant influences on the type and presentation of deceptive messages. Finally, studies using this procedure typically involve strangers; hence, they offer few insights about relational deception.

Overall, we deem this procedure to be highly ethical and find it relatively easy to use. It is nonthreatening and places the participants at minimal risk. Because data collection procedures are simple, this approach appears to be relatively efficient. Although it remains a popular technique, we have serious questions about its utility for investigating deceptive communication. Though it was instrumental in laying the foundation for research in this area, we believe other available procedures provide a more realistic assessment of deceptive transactions.

Reaction Assessments

Ekman and Friesen were among the first scholars in social psychology to study deception. Their early studies relied on a procedure we label *reaction assessments.* In Chapter 2, we described how Ekman and Friesen (1974) requested nursing students to provide truthful and deceptive reactions to a series of pleasant and unpleasant slides they were shown.

To heighten their motivation to deceive effectively, the nursing students were told that their ability to conceal their emotional reactions when working with patients was a requirement for their profession. In fact, they were told that "skilled members of their profession" were successful deceivers in similar studies. Truthful and deceptive reactions to the slides were videotaped and shown to a separate set of research participants who made judgments of honesty and deceit.

Several variations of this procedure appear in the literature. Hocking, Bouchner, Kaminski, and Miller (1979) used similar procedures, but solicited criminal justice majors to participate in the study. The criminal justice majors were told that the ability to deceive effectively would assist them in their careers and that the results of their performance would be forwarded to the criminal justice department. Stiff, Kim, and Ramesh (1992) asked relational partners to reveal or conceal their actual emotional reactions to pleasant (scenes from Yellowstone National Park) and unpleasant (scenes from the movie, *The Faces of Death*) film clips. In both studies, these videotaped interviews were shown to a separate group of respondents who made veracity judgments.

This general procedure has several features that recommend it. First, participants in these studies were motivated to "perform well" when asked to conceal their emotions. Second, these videotaped interviews can be used for several purposes. Similar to the *single message presentation* procedure, videotapes permit a thorough analysis of the verbal and nonverbal behaviors associated with truth and deception. The same videotapes can also be shown to observers to investigate factors influencing judgments of honesty and deceit.

This procedure is not without its limitations. Deception is sanctioned by the experimenter who instructs participants about when to lie and to tell the truth. Although the motivation to deceive effectively may be high, the motivation of observers who watch the videotapes and make veracity judgments is often relatively low. The procedure also heightens the anticipation of deception by observers who are asked to identify truthful and deceptive messages. Hence, findings about judgments of veracity may lack generalizability to more natural settings. Finally, interview questions are scripted, reflecting a linear conceptualization of the deception process and preventing an assessment of the interactive nature of deception.

Though the reaction assessments procedure is somewhat more cumbersome than the uninterrupted message presentation procedure, it remains relatively easy to use. Furthermore, this procedure meets guidelines for ethical research provided that the experiment is fully explained to participants following the session, including a statement that their performance will *not* be made available to others. The advantage of this procedure over the single message stems from its attempt to heighten motivation for people to deceive effectively.

The Exline Procedure

Perhaps the most creative approach to studying deception in laboratory settings was developed by Exline and his colleagues. In Chapter 2 we described how this procedure is used to implicate research participants in a cheating incident during an experimental task. After the task is completed, participants are asked to answer a few questions about their performance, and face the decision of "coming clean" and admitting their dishonesty or responding deceptively in hopes of avoiding detection.

Although the Exline procedure is quite involved, its favorable characteristics make it a popular choice among deception scholars (Bauchner et al., 1977; Bauchner et al., 1980; deTurck & Miller, 1985; Exline et al., 1970; Stiff & Miller, 1986). One of the most appealing aspects of the Exline procedure is its production of deceptive behavior that is not sanctioned by the experimenter. Participants in these studies decided to communicate deceptively and faced important consequences if their deception was detected. Unlike most procedures, the Exline procedure places the responsibility for deception squarely on the shoulders of deceivers.

A second feature of this procedure stems from the heightened motivation of participants to deceive effectively. The negative consequences of cheating during an experiment, associated with the incentives for outstanding performance offered by some researchers (deTurck & Miller, 1985; Stiff & Miller, 1986), motivate deceivers to avoid detection. In fact, one criticism of our use of the procedure was that it may have been "too motivating" for participants (Stiff & Miller, 1986).

In addition, videotapes of these truthful and deceptive interviews can be analyzed for nonverbal content (deTurck & Miller, 1985; Exline et al., 1970; Stiff & Miller, 1986) and shown to a separate group of participants who are asked to make veracity judgments (Bauchner et al., 1977; Stiff & Miller, 1986). Thus this procedure is effective for studying verbal and nonverbal deceptive behavior as well as factors that are related to observers' veracity judgments.

Major criticisms of the Exline procedure involve ethical questions about the use of human research participants. Great care must be taken to ensure that participants are "given the opportunity" to cheat but are not coerced into doing so. Unfortunately, our experience has been that most undergraduate students are eager to cheat once the confederate suggests duplicity (about 90%). In one of our studies two participants initiated the discussion of cheating and attempted to convince the confederate to cheat on the task! Following the procedure, very careful debriefing procedures are necessary to ensure that participants feel good about themselves and their role in the experiment. In most cases, these discussions are quite successful. Nevertheless, this procedure requires constant attention to the rights of participants and the ethical obligations of researchers.

The Exline procedure is not useful for studying relational deception. It does not conceptualize deception as a transactional process, although Stiff and Miller (1986) moved in this direction by varying the extent to which the interviewer indicated belief in the interviewee's answers. Participants who are asked to judge veracity do not participate in the interview and are thus often relatively unmotivated to make accurate judgments. In addition, instructions provided to these participants often heighten their anticipation of deception above levels found in many natural settings.

Relational Interviews

One procedure has been popular for studying deception among relational partners. Comadena (1982) was one of the first researchers to focus on possible differences in deception and detection between intimate relational partners and friends. Relational partners were asked to arrive at the lab with a friend in tow. The friend and one relational partner took turns interviewing the other partner as he or she described the factual and emotional content of several film clips. The interviews were unstructured and provided the basis for veracity judgments made by interviewees.

Several recent studies used a similar procedure (Levine & McCornack, 1992; McCornack & Parks, 1986; Stiff, Kim, & Ramesh, 1992). Although these studies did not focus on behavioral correlates of deception, videotaped recordings and transcripts of these interviews can be effectively used to investigate verbal and nonverbal behavior (Stiff, Corman, & Raghavendra, 1991; Stiff, Kim, & Ramesh, 1992).

The relational interview procedure has proven quite effective for studying relational deception. It is fairly unobtrusive and unlikely to influence the relationship, a prominent concern when investigating relational communication. This procedure is effective for studying deception detection as well as the verbal and nonverbal correlates of deception. In addition, the procedure conceptualizes deception as a transactional process, though only two studies (Stiff et al., 1991; Stiff, Corman et al., 1992) investigated the mutual influence of deceivers and deceivees on the deception process.

A major limitation of this approach stems from the fact that deception is sanctioned by the experimenter. Motivation is also a potential problem, although we have found that "challenging" friends and relational partners to deceive effectively and to detect deception often heightens their motivation to perform well. Such challenges also heighten suspicion and may limit the generalizability of ensuing veracity judgments. In fact, variations of this general procedure have been employed to investigate the influence of "aroused suspicion" on relational deception (McCornack & Parks, 1986; Stiff, Kim, & Ramesh, 1992).

Simulated Interviews

A novel approach to studying veracity judgments was recently introduced to the deception literature (Stiff et al., 1989). We were interested in the information processing patterns that lead observers to rely on either nonverbal behaviors or verbal content when making judgments of truth and deception. Given our interest in information processing rather than deception detection, per se, it was unnecessary to expose observers to actual truthful and deceptive messages. Instead, we scripted a series of interviews controlling the visual, vocal, and verbal cues of interviewees (paid actors) as they responded to an interviewer's questions.

Relying on findings from prior research, we identified several visual, vocal, and verbal cues typically associated with deception (see Chapter 4 for a complete discussion of these behaviors). We instructed the actors to display many (deception conditions) or few (truthful conditions) of these cues when responding to the interviewer's questions. For example, one interview that manipulated truthful visual behavior, deceptive vocal behavior, and deceptive verbal content required actors to display few of the visual behaviors associated with deception (e.g., broken eye contact and posture shifts), many of the vocal behaviors associated with deception (e.g., audible pauses and sentence repairs), and many of the verbal content cues characteristic of deceptive messages (e.g., vague and inconsistent responses). Each actor created eight interviews, one for each combination of truthful and deceptive visual, vocal, and verbal cues.

These interviews concerned a cheating incident that occurred during a recent exam, with the interviewer playing the role of an instructor talking to each of the students in the class to determine who cheated and who did not. These videotaped interviews, along with background information about the situation, were shown to observers who made veracity judgments and provided evaluations of the visual, vocal, and verbal behaviors.

This procedure is unique because it cannot answer questions about deception or deception detection accuracy. Instead, its utility is limited to investigations of factors influencing judgments people make. By manipulating the behavior of message sources, researchers can isolate specific combinations of verbal and nonverbal cues that influence veracity judgments. For example, one of our studies found that people relied almost exclusively on nonverbal behavior to make judgments of deception even though they were able to identify accurately characteristics of truthful and deceptive verbal content.

While this procedure is useful for answering questions about deceptive judgments, it has limited application for a broad range of questions about the deception process. For example, it is not useful for assessing relational deception, or the verbal and nonverbal correlates of deception. The procedure provides little motivation for observers who are asked to make judgments about veracity, and it does not conceptualize deception as a transactional process. The procedure is also likely to heighten the anticipation of deception among participants who make veracity judgments. On the other hand, this procedure is unlikely to raise any serious ethical questions about the use of human research participants.

Survey Interviews

Perhaps the most straightforward method for studying deception was employed by Miller, Mongeau, and Sleight (1984). Instead of structuring a deceptive interaction and observing it, they chose to ask people about prior experiences with deception and deception detection. Using survey interview procedures, they asked people to recall prior deception experiences with a relational partner and with a stranger. Respondents reported behaviors that signaled deception in others, as well as those they attempted to control when deceiving others.

Survey responses were analyzed and provided the foundation for several generalizations about differences between relational deception and deception among strangers. The intriguing feature of this procedure is its simplicity. Perhaps the best way to learn about deception is to ask people to describe the deceptive transactions they have with others.

Although this procedure does not involve direct observation of truthful and deceptive behavior, people's responses reflect deception as it occurs in natural contexts. Thus observations made using this procedure reflect the levels of motivation and suspicion typical of natural deceptive transactions. In addition, much of the deception described in these survey responses was not sanctioned by a third party. The procedure also permits investigation of relational deception, as well as deception among strangers.

As useful as interview procedures may be for investigating people's *perceptions* of truthful and deceptive behaviors, as well as their reports of behaviors they rely on to detect deception, such procedures may not be optimal for investigating *actual* behaviors associated with deceptive behavior and veracity judgments. Although observation of deception does not occur, interview questions can be developed to reflect a transactional conceptualization of deception.

The validity of this procedure rests on the assumption that respondents are willing and able to provide accurate information about their communicative behavior. While some may question the validity of this assumption, and avoid this research procedure, our belief is that respondents sometimes may be able to offer reasonably accurate accounts of their own behaviors that are not observable in more controlled laboratory settings. As such, we view this procedure as one useful alternative for studying deceptive transactions.

Interaction Analysis

The most recent development has been the use of *interaction analysis* to describe truthful and deceptive messages. Interaction analysis involves systematic examination of segments of communicative transactions. These interaction segments are sometimes as small as a speaking turn in a conversation, or sometimes a thought unit within a turn. Once the interaction has been segmented, coders are asked to evaluate each segment using a previously developed and validated coding scheme. Each segment of the interaction is assigned a numerical value representing a specific characteristic of interest. For example, Bavelas and her colleagues (Bavelas et al., 1990) developed a measure of equivocation and used it to study deception. They asked coders to read responses people provided to various questions and to evaluate the degree of equivocation in each response. Bavelas et al. assigned numerical values to the ratings and used these values to draw statistical comparisons among different categories of messages.

Other researchers have used similar procedures to isolate verbal features of truthful and deceptive messages. Stiff, Kim, and Ramesh (1992) used transcripts of truthful and deceptive interactions to assess the level of "cognitive involvement" reflected in an interviewer's questions and examine whether this involvement was related to subsequent veracity judgments. Stiff et al. (1991) used interaction analysis procedures to identify directive-reply patterns in truthful and deceptive interactions. This later investigation also identified the relationship between different forms of interviewer requests for information and the *nonverbal* behaviors of respondents.

The data necessary for interaction analysis can take many forms. Stiff et al. (1991) used transcripts from truthful and deceptive interviews, while Bavelas et al. (1990) studied equivocation using videotaped recordings of interaction. We recently began a project that applies interaction analysis procedures to investigative forensic interviews of child abuse victims. Because these interviews are routinely recorded for evidentiary purposes, they provide a rich source of information for investigating verbal behavior. After identifying a sample of truthful and deceptive interviews from relevant case data, we plan to use interaction analysis to isolate specific question and response patterns that characterize truthful and deceptive interviews. This procedure can also be used to isolate patterns of interaction that influence veracity judgments made by investigators.

Although interaction analysis is a viable method for conducting micro-level analyses of truthful and deceptive transactions, the quality of the analysis rests on the quality of interactions being analyzed. In this regard, the criteria presented earlier in this chapter are useful for assessing the validity of this research procedure.

The procedure clearly characterizes deception as a transactional process, and has a number of favorable attributes that are largely missing in other procedures. One compelling advantage of this procedure is that it is not limited to laboratory observations. Interaction analysis of naturally occurring interviews allows researchers to study deception in contexts where people are motivated to lie (or tell the truth) effectively and apt to suspect deception when it occurs. More important, deception investigated using interaction analysis is not sanctioned by investigators. Finally, interaction analysis typically permits the investigation of both verbal and nonverbal behavior.

Interaction analysis is limited by the degree to which researchers can accurately separate truthful and deceptive interactions. In many naturally occurring interactions it may be impossible to distinguish truthful and deceptive interactions accurately. However, in some interactions, relevant casework may provide enough information for researchers to confidently categorize the interaction as probably truthful or probably deceptive. Nevertheless, without accurate categorization, comparisons among interactions have limited utility.

Concerns about the privacy of participants in these interviews raise questions about the ethical implications of their use for research purposes, and we will have more to say about this issue in Chapter 7. These concerns and the labor-intensive nature of the method render interaction analysis a seldom-used procedure in deception research. However, given the advantages of studying deception as it naturally occurs, we view interaction analysis as one important procedural alternative for scholars of deceptive communication.

SUMMARY AND CONCLUSIONS

The procedures evaluated in this chapter represent a cross-section of designs employed by deception researchers. It bears mentioning that many deception studies employ variations of these general procedures, and some studies effectively combine features of different research procedures.

We offer this analysis to summarize the choices available to researchers, and to underscore our contention that no single procedure is superior for drawing conclusions about the deception process. Rather than debating the relative merits of specific procedures, we prefer to use a variety of different procedures in our research. If we employ a single "research paradigm" for studying deception, then we must always question the extent to which our conclusions are an artifact of the procedures we used, rather than the process we investigated. Only when different procedures produce similar findings can we become confident that our conclusions reflect deceptive transactions as they naturally occur. In this regard, our most confident recommendation is for scholars to employ a variety of different procedures in their research programs.

4

Characteristics of Deceptive Behavior

Research on deceptive communication has traditionally followed one of two conceptually related paths. Many scholars have sought to uncover verbal and nonverbal clues to deception (see Cody et al., 1984; Knapp et al., 1974, for examples). This approach assumes that once clues to deceit have been identified, people can use them in everyday interactions to distinguish truthful communicators from prevaricators. For example, participants in our studies often tell us that they look for indirect eye contact and nervous behavior when they suspect deception. If research can verify that these behaviors are valid indices of deceit, then we can rely on them more confidently to make veracity judgments.

A second path in the deception literature has been followed by individuals interested in deception detection. These researchers (see Kraut, 1978; Stiff & Miller, 1986, for examples) seek to identify factors that enhance or inhibit people's ability to detect deception. Their eventual goal is to specify personal characteristics, situations, and relationships that influence the ability to detect deception. In this chapter we will delve into the research on verbal and nonverbal behaviors. The following two chapters will examine people's ability to detect deception accurately and identify factors that influence judgments of deception.

EMPHASIS ON NONVERBAL BEHAVIOR

To reemphasize an earlier point, research on cues associated with deception has stressed nonverbal behavior. Only a handful of studies have tried to identify the verbal correlates of deception and deceptive judgments. We offer two explanations for this emphasis on nonverbal behavior: historical foundations and a lack of adequate theories to guide research. The pioneers of deception research were primarily physiologists and social psychologists, and their efforts paved the way for those who followed this line of research. The physiologists wanted to develop machines to trap deceptive communicators. Research on the polygraph has focused heavily on physiological changes accompanying deceptive messages (for reviews see Lykken, 1974; Wade & Orne, 1981). These researchers were only interested in communication insofar as it triggered certain physiological responses.

Paul Ekman and his colleagues were among the first social psychologists to study deception. Being students of nonverbal behavior, they focused exclusively on vocal and visual cues that are present during deception. In fact, their "leakage hypothesis," which was developed to explain the deception process, exclusively concerns nonverbal behaviors that are difficult to control and that are often "leaked" during deception (Ekman & Friesen, 1969, 1974). Questions posed by these early investigators set the stage for subsequent research programs. As a result, most of the deception research conducted by social psychologists has evidenced a continuing interest in nonverbal behavior.

Knapp and his colleagues (Knapp et al., 1974) were the first communication researchers to study deception, and in doing so, they stressed the role of both verbal and nonverbal behavior in deceptive transactions. Since then, several other researchers have looked at the role of verbal content in deception and deception detection (Cody et al., 1984; Kraut, 1978; Stiff & Miller, 1986; Wagner & Pease, 1976). It is noteworthy that research on these cues has been restricted to either holistic assessments or isolation of very general characteristics of verbal behavior.

A second explanation for the emphasis on nonverbal behaviors relates to the shortage of fruitful theories about deceptive communication. Much of the research has not been theory-driven; unlike many other areas of inquiry, students of deception have failed to identify and develop a dominant theoretical perspective. Instead, early researchers focused on more practical pursuits such as identifying behaviors that would distinguish liars from truth-tellers. Lacking an adequate theoretical foundation, researchers depended largely on commonsense observations to guide their work.

Conventional wisdom and cultural stereotypes suggest that by "looking someone straight in the eye" one can detect deceit in all save the most polished liars. No doubt such folk wisdom led to a concern with nonverbal behaviors at the expense of verbal content. This influence of nonverbal behavior is still evident today. Though recent theoretical developments point to a promising research future, the vast majority of deception studies continue to emphasize nonverbal behaviors.

THEORETICAL EXPLANATIONS OF DECEPTIVE BEHAVIOR

Before examining the theoretical explanations for verbal and nonverbal behavioral correlates of deception, we must restate the importance of *intentionality* in our definition of deception. As we discussed in Chapter 2, some scholars have abandoned a source-based definition of deception in favor of a linguistic definition (Bavelas et al., 1990). We argued that once we abandon the concept of communicator intent, we also abandon the theoretical underpinnings of deceptive behavior.

The arousal associated with fear of detection and the cognitive effort required to design effective deceptive messages are two theoretically grounded processes that predict behavioral differences between truthful and deceptive communicators. The underlying rationale for heightened arousal and increased cognitive effort stems from the communicator's intention to mislead. Without this intent, it is unlikely that inaccurate messages (honest mistakes) would require additional cognitive effort or increase a communicator's arousal. With this distinction in mind, we proceed with a review of two prominent theoretical explanations for differences between truthful and deceptive behavior.

Arousal Theory

Psychophysiological research on lie detection illustrates how arousal theory has been used to investigate nonverbal behaviors associated with deception. As early as 1929, Chappell argued the mere knowledge that one is lying is enough to induce arousal. In 1963, Gustafson and Orne (1963) contended that the fear of possible punishment produces heightened arousal in liars. Since that time, this anticipated linkage between lying and arousal has resulted in considerable research aimed at developing mechanical devices such as polygraphs and voice stress analyzers to detect lying (for reviews, see Lykken, 1974; Wade & Orne, 1981). The accuracy and utility of these devices have prompted considerable debate both among researchers and among concerned professionals and laypersons in other areas—consider for instance, the many issues surrounding the use of polygraphs as courtroom evidence. We will not enter into this rhetorical fray in this chapter. Instead, we will review some of the literature relevant to the theoretical linkage between physiological arousal and nonverbal behaviors.

In questioning the validity of polygraph examinations, Lykken (1978) distinguished between two polygraph procedures used to assess veracity. One procedure involves two examiners, one who administers the test and one who "blindly" scores responses to it. A second procedure permits a single examiner to administer the test and to score the responses. This second procedure incorporates more "global" estimates of veracity in addition to the physiological data provided by the machine. Lykken argues that this second procedure allows judgments to be influenced by extra-polygraphic (visual and vocal nonverbal) cues. Polygraph exams are often quite lengthy, including several verbal exchanges between the examiner and the respondent. Lengthy exams provide the opportunity for respondents to display many extra-polygraphic cues that can influence the scoring of the physiological output. For example, examiners confronted with ambiguous polygraph output will likely judge the respondent deceptive if he or she was fidgety and did not maintain eye contact during the test. Conversely, ambiguous output might be interpreted as truthful if the respondent's body movements were more natural and relaxed.

The combination of these extra-polygraphic (nonverbal) cues with physiological output enhances an examiner's ability to judge veracity when compared to the results a "blind" scorer might achieve (Lykken, 1978, p. 138). Stated differently, the presence of nonverbal behaviors associated with physiological responses significantly increases the accuracy of polygraph examinations.

The Lykken study suggests a close tie between physiological arousal and nonverbal behavior. The presence of nonverbal cues, produced by heightened arousal, facilitates detection accuracy. Knapp et al. (1974) were among the first communication scholars to invoke arousal as a theoretical foundation for studying nonverbal behaviors associated with deception. Implicitly or explicitly, this is the predominant posture of most deception researchers.

Though arousal is thought to hinder the success of most deceivers, it bears mentioning that heightened arousal may facilitate the act of deception for some people. In addition, pathological liars may not experience the heightened arousal that most "normal" deceivers experience. While these individual differences are distributed among the participants of most deception investigations, few studies have investigated the moderating role of personality on the relationship between arousal and deceptive message production.

One shortcoming of arousal theory is the rather weak link between nonverbal behaviors and various sources of arousal (Miller, Sleight, & deTurck, 1989). Situational contexts play a key role in the interpretation of arousal-induced behavior and in many situations it is often assumed that arousal-induced behavior is indicative of deception. Unfortunately, a number of alternative sources of arousal may exist. For example, the prospect of being labeled a liar, whether accurately or inaccurately, can heighten arousal and produce the types of nonverbal behaviors often associated with deception. Moreover, some people are consistently highly aroused because of such characteristics as shyness or lack of confidence, and these persons often exhibit arousal cues when they are being perfectly candid. Simply put, nervous behavior is not necessarily deceptive behavior.

A study by deTurck & Miller (1985) questioned the validity of the arousal explanation. Using the Exline procedure, described in Chapter 2, and a device to measure skin resistance, they measured the physiological arousal of students who responded truthfully or deceptively to questions about performance on an assigned task. As expected, the arousal level of truth-tellers was significantly lower than the level of deceivers. A third group of students was bombarded periodically with "white noise" as they responded truthfully to the interview questions, a procedure used to heighten their arousal to the same level experienced by deceivers.

Comparison of nonverbal behaviors exhibited by deceivers, unaroused truth-tellers, and aroused truth-tellers produced some interesting findings. Six cues: adaptors, hand gestures, speech errors, pauses, response latency, and message duration, distinguished deceivers from unaroused truth-tellers. Most intriguingly, however, these same cues distinguished deceivers from aroused truth-tellers. Because the levels of arousal between deceivers and aroused truth-tellers were comparable, deTurck and Miller concluded that the nonverbal behaviors displayed by deceivers apparently are not due to arousal per se, but rather are unique to deception-induced arousal (p. 197). These results suggest that the motivational source of deception-induced arousal (i.e., fear of being detected) may produce nonverbal behaviors differing from the behaviors produced by other arousal sources. Clearly, arousal in the absence of deception was insufficient to produce the nonverbal behaviors displayed by deceivers. This discrepancy, along with other ambiguities, has led to the development of an alternative theoretical position to investigate the verbal and nonverbal correlates of deception.

Cognitive Theory

Cody and his colleagues were among the first deception researchers to examine cognition's role in the production of deceptive messages. These authors argued that effective deceptive messages require more cognitive effort to produce than truthful messages. To develop believable lies, deceivers must first construct messages that are consistent with existing facts and are thus plausible substitutes for the truth. Furthermore, subsequent messages must be monitored closely to ensure they are consistent and that they plausibly extend and clarify previous statements.

This increased cognitive effort should manifest itself in the form of specific verbal and nonverbal cues (Cody et al., 1984; Miller & Burgoon, 1982). Indeed, Cody et al. identified a number of vocal cues (e.g., pause duration, response length, response latency, speech errors) and verbal cues (e.g., number of specific references, number of nonspecific references, number of temporal references) that separated truth-tellers from liars.

In addition to its potential theoretical advantages, the cognitive approach adopted by Cody et al. (1984) may serve to redirect the efforts of deception researchers. Specifically, the cognitive explanation attaches more importance to the vocal and verbal components of deceptive behavior and reduces attention to the visual components. We agree with Cody et al. (1984) that this redirection may prove productive by highlighting the crucial role of verbal behavior in the process of deception.

ISOLATING VERBAL AND NONVERBAL BEHAVIOR

Before proceeding with a discussion of the verbal and nonverbal correlates of deception and deceptive judgments, we will briefly describe the procedures researchers typically use to identify and to measure these behaviors. We begin by discussing visual and vocal cues commonly investigated in deception research and end by examining a number of verbal cues that have been investigated.

Visual and Vocal Cues

Although the number of verbal and nonverbal cues one could investigate seems countless, researchers generally agree about the visual and vocal cues that are particularly important. This consensus emerges from reviews of the literature on nonverbal correlates of deception and judgments of deception (Zuckerman, DePaulo, & Rosenthal, 1981; Zuckerman

& Driver, 1985). A representative list of the cues we have used in much of our research, along with their definitions, is presented in Table 4.1.

The typical procedure used to isolate these cues involves a comparison of truthful and deceptive messages. After generating these messages, researchers ask raters to code a number of verbal and nonverbal behaviors in each message. Statistical comparisons identify cues that vary across truthful and deceptive messages. Cues that are present more frequently in deceptive than in truthful messages are positively correlated with deception, while those that are found more often in truthful messages are negatively correlated.

Trained coders analyzing one cue at a time typically produce intercoder correlations above .85. As would be expected, some cues are more difficult to code resulting in somewhat lower reliability estimates. For example, eye blinks and indirect eye gaze are often more difficult to code reliably than adaptors and posture shifts.[1] When analyzing our data, we routinely convert the scores for most nonverbal cues to rates by dividing by the response length. This procedure provides an estimate of the amount of nonverbal activity per minute of response time, an important consideration given the variance in response time across liars and truth-tellers.

Two cues investigated in many deception studies, voice pitch and pupil dilation (Zuckerman et al., 1981), have been omitted from our research because they are difficult to measure effectively in ongoing interactions. Although voice pitch and pupil dilation may be useful micro indicators of deception, these are difficult to detect on videotape, and conversational participants may have difficulty consciously recognizing them as they occur. Thus, for the most part, our investigations have primarily focused on cues that can be readily perceived by conversational participants and third-party observers who serve as coders.

Verbal Cues

Given the few studies that have investigated verbal correlates, there is less agreement about the important specific characteristics of verbal content. Two types of verbal cues have received the lion's share of attention in prior research. Three studies (Cody et al., 1984; Knapp et al., 1974; Stiff & Miller, 1986) have investigated specific verbal characteristics of deceptive messages (Table 4.2).

Because the situations that provide the basis for truthful and deceptive statements vary across studies, it is difficult to identify an optimal set of verbal cues for all deceptive transactions. For example, Cody et al. (1984) had respondents lie about their favorite vacation spots. Cody

TABLE 4.1

Nonverbal Cues Investigated in Deception Research

Visual Cues

Adaptors: The amount of time either hand is moving while touching the body during the response.

Hand Gestures: The amount of time either hand is moving while not touching the body during the response.

Indirect Eye Gaze: The amount of time spent not meeting the interviewer's eyes while answering questions or making statements.

Broken Eye Contact: The number of times eye contact is established and broken during a response.

Eye Blinks: The number of eye blinks during the response.

Smile Duration: The amount of time spent smiling during the response. A smile occurs when the corners of the mouth are turned upward.

Posture Shifts: The number of times the trunk of the body is shifted during the response.

Leg/Foot Movements: The amount of time either leg or foot is moving during the response.

Vocal Cues

Audible Pauses: The number of times a pause is filled with sounds like "err," "umm," "aah," "ya know," etc., during the response.

Silent Pauses: The amount of silent time that occurs once the subject has started to answer a question or make a statement.

Sentence Repairs: The number of times a sentence or phrase is started, interrupted, and then repeated during a response.

Response Latency: The amount of time between the end of an interviewer's question and the beginning of the subject's response.

Response Length: The amount of total time (speaking and silent) from the beginning of a response to the end of a response.

---

and his colleagues coded verbal references to specific actions, specific persons, descriptions of persons, temporal references, and specific places that were present in truthful and deceptive messages. The Stiff and Miller (1986) study, on the other hand, involved deception about cheating in a situation where participants were awarded $50 for outstanding task performance. Verbal cues such as statements of personal, other, and mutual responsibility, and the number of self-, other-, and mutual references were coded for truthful and deceptive messages. It would have made no sense to code these cues in the Cody et al. study, because the likelihood of such references in their situation was low.

TABLE 4.2

Verbal Cues Investigated in Deception Research

Self-References: The number of times a subject refers to himself or herself during a response.

Other-References: The number of times a subject refers to others during a response.

Mutual References: The number of times a subject mutually refers to himself or herself and others during a response.

Statements of Personal Responsibility: The number of statements in which a subject assumes personal responsibility for an event or outcome during a response (i.e., "It was my idea"; "I was the one in charge"; "I guess it was my fault").

Statements of Other Responsibility: The number of statements in which a subject assigns responsibility for an event or outcome to others (i.e., "I wasn't the one who came up with the idea"; "I was just following the others").

Statements of Mutual Responsibility: The number of statements in which a subject indicates that responsibility for an event or outcome should be shared by himself or herself and at least one other person ("We all were a little to blame"; "it was my fault as much as it was theirs"; "we all should get the credit for this").

Factual Statements: Statements about people, objects, or events that, in principle, are verifiable. These statements do not have to be true, only verifiable ("I studied 5 hours last night"; "The size of the group has been steadily increasing").

Hypothetical Statements: Statements that refer to a situation or event that has not occurred, but has some probability of occurring (i.e., "If I get the raise, then I will probably work harder"; "People would have responded differently to another leader").

Opinion Statements: Statements in which the subject indicates his or her own opinion about some person, object, or event ("I would prefer to do things differently"; "I don't like situations like this").

NOTE: It is possible for a statement to fit more than one category.

Kraut (1978) and Stiff and Miller (1986) pursued a second approach to coding verbal content by asking raters to make holistic assessments of the plausibility, concreteness, consistency, clarity, and conciseness of truthful and deceptive verbal statements. These variables were found to be highly intercorrelated and were collapsed into a single factor for analysis (Stiff & Miller, 1986). These assessments are generally less time-consuming than coding specific features of verbal content, and they provide an overall impression of the verbal content not gleaned by an analysis of specific cues.

We recommend using both approaches. The former provides more detail and produces data that are amenable to sequential analyses, while the latter provides the type of holistic assessment individuals probably make before arriving at judgments of honesty and deceit. In either case, it is imperative that verbal content be coded from written transcripts of interactions. Without the help of transcripts, coders are likely to confound characteristics of verbal, vocal, and visual content in their assessments.

NONVERBAL CORRELATES OF DECEPTION

Though the label "nonverbal correlates of deception" commonly appears in the deception literature, it is something of a misnomer. Because the phrase is typically used to refer to cues differentiating truthful and deceptive behaviors, a more accurate label is "verbal and nonverbal correlates of truth *and* deception."

This distinction is important because our labels often reflect the way we think about issues. Though most researchers are concerned with the implications of their findings for deception detection, research can also be helpful in studying truth detection. In other words, investigations of deception are also investigations of truthfulness: The truth and a lie may usefully be thought of as opposite sides of the same behavioral coin.

A review of research on the behavioral correlates of truth and deception reveals numerous, often conflicting conclusions. Several methodological issues make it difficult to provide a comprehensive summary of the nonverbal correlates of deception. Two of these issues, the file drawer problem and procedural differences, are discussed below.

Methodological Limitations

The File Drawer Problem. The "file drawer problem" concerns a relatively simple issue: Do published studies about deception adequately represent the entire body of deception research (published and unpublished) or do published studies furnish us with a biased assessment of the deception process?

Every researcher is aware of the low publication rates in national and regional journals. Some studies do not measure up to publication standards, and many that do never make it into press. Competently conducted studies that do not produce "interesting" results are typically bypassed in favor of those that do. Studies reporting null findings are not published as frequently as those reporting statistically significant effects. This is particularly true in research areas lacking fully developed theories. When research is theory driven, null findings are often deemed interesting, especially if they disconfirm the theory, but such credibility is rarely conferred on null findings when research is not theory driven.

Because theory development in deception has been sparse, a number of research reports finding no correlation between nonverbal cues and deceptive behavior have probably been consigned to the file drawers of researchers. To our knowledge, a study we conducted (Stiff & Miller, 1986) provides the only example of published research in which none of the reported nonverbal cues were correlated with actual deception. Although these results were probably perceived as the least interesting aspect of the study by the reviewers, we are left wondering how many other studies produced similar results and were never published. Are our findings that unique, or were we fortunate to have more interesting additional findings that warranted publication in the eyes of the reviewers?

Not only may some entire studies producing null results be gathering dust, authors of some published articles may also have selectively reported only those cues associated with deception. Those cues that were coded but not correlated with deception may have been omitted from the text because they were deemed unimportant. Such decisions are perhaps justified given the nature of the review process, but they also result in an "overreporting" of significant findings and leave readers with a false impression of the relationship between nonverbal behaviors and deception.

Though speculative, the possibility of a file drawer problem necessitates caution when interpreting the relationship between nonverbal cues and deception: If the problem exists, then the relationship between certain nonverbal cues and deception may be overstated. With this in mind, let us turn to another methodological issue that limits our ability to draw confident conclusions about the nonverbal correlates of deception.

Procedural Differences. Procedural differences among studies produce variations in nonverbal cues that are correlated with deception, and in turn, these variations impact on informed discussion of the behavioral correlates of deception. One important difference involves the context in which deception occurs. In many studies deception is requested and sanctioned by the experimenter. For example, the procedures of the Cody et al. (1984) study involved a request for participants to lie about their favorite vacation spots during an interview. Other studies (deTurck & Miller, 1985; Stiff & Miller, 1986) relied on the Exline procedure in which respondents lied to an interviewer without the consent of the experimenter and in hopes of avoiding the negative consequences of cheating during an experimental task. Although both procedures have their advantages and limitations, motivation to avoid detection in studies using the Exline procedure is likely to be much greater than in studies where deception is requested and sanctioned by the experimenter. These differences in motivation are likely to produce different nonverbal correlates across studies.

The hypothesized effect of motivation on behavioral correlates of deception produces a mixed bag of possible outcomes. On one hand, people highly motivated to avoid detection are likely to work harder and to monitor their own behavior more closely than people who are minimally motivated. On the other hand, increased motivation should produce heightened arousal thus resulting in the display of more nonverbal behaviors associated with deception. This latter possibility was evidenced by DePaulo, Stone, and Lassiter (1985) who found that participants in a variety of highly motivating situations produced less convincing deceptive messages than participants in less motivating situations.

A second methodological difference among prior studies concerns the amount of time participants have to plan their deceptions. Some studies (DePaulo, Davis, & Lanier, 1980; Miller et al., 1983) manipulated opportunities to plan by allowing some participants time to rehearse and requiring others to deceive spontaneously. Investigations that have not explicitly manipulated the opportunity for preparation can be differentiated by reading the study procedures to identify the amount of time allowed for planning.

Given an opportunity to anticipate questions and to rehearse answers, some deceivers should display fewer nonverbal correlates associated with deception. For example, one might hypothesize that planned deceptive messages have shorter response latencies and fewer speech errors than spontaneous ones. Once again, however, a mixed bag possibility arises, for while some deceivers may profit from planning time, others may actually suffer in their attempts to lie effectively (Miller et al., 1983).

The influence of these procedural differences on nonverbal behavior should not be underestimated. In the next section, we present an overall summary of nonverbal correlates of deception. This summary is followed by a discussion of the effects of motivation to deceive and the opportunity to rehearse on nonverbal communicative behaviors.

Findings on Nonverbal Correlates of Deception

Overall Analysis. Zuckerman and Driver (1985) extended the work of Zuckerman et al. (1981) by conducting a meta-analytic review of studies investigating the nonverbal correlates of deception. Meta-analytic reviews employ statistical procedures that permit the results of many different studies to be cumulated into a single set of statistics representing the findings of an entire body of literature.

Zuckerman and Driver (1985) identify five visual cues that have emerged as consistent correlates of deception across studies: pupil dilation, blinking, facial segmentation, adaptors, and bodily segmentation. Of these cues, only two, blinking and adaptors, are of much practical utility for deception detection and both were positively associated with deception. Although pupil dilation can be measured, it is not possible to do so during everyday deceptive transactions. The two remaining visual correlates, facial segmentation and bodily segmentation, are vague and lack clear conceptual meaning. Thus, of the 12 visual cues included in the Zuckerman & Driver (1985) review, only 2 were practically useful and consistent correlates of deception. This finding is surprising when one recalls the emphasis placed on visual behavior by both researchers and ordinary communicators.

Of the six vocal cues included in the overall analysis (Zuckerman & Driver, 1985), four were consistently related to deception across all studies: response length, speech errors, speech hesitations, and voice pitch. Compared to truthful messages, deceptive messages are characterized by shorter response lengths, a higher speech pitch, more speech errors, and more speech hesitations.

These results suggest that investigation of vocal nonverbal cues as correlates of deception may be a more fruitful path to follow than the traditional emphasis that has been placed on visual cues. Roughly 17% of the commonly studied visual cues have been identified as consistent correlates of deception while 50% of the vocal cues have produced positive results.

Effects of Motivation. Zuckerman and Driver (1985) also investigated the influence of motivation on nonverbal correlates of deception. Studies used in the overall analysis were divided into high and low motivation groups, and meta-analyses were conducted for the studies in each subgroup.

Comparisons between the subgroups indicate a number of differences in the cues identified as correlates of deception. Highly motivated deceivers displayed significantly fewer head movements, blinks, posture shifts, and less direct eye gaze than deceivers with relatively low motivation. In addition, highly motivated deceivers produced significantly shorter responses, slower speech rates, and higher voice pitch than their low motivation counterparts.

Effects of Planning. Similar meta-analytic procedures were used to examine the effects of planning on nonverbal correlates of deception.

Each study was placed into one of three subgroups (high, medium, and low planning time) based on the amount of time participants were given to plan and to rehearse their deceptions.

Unlike motivation, planning had little influence on the nonverbal correlates of deception. Cues that were correlates of deception among studies in the high planning subgroup were also correlates in the low and moderate subgroups. Although significant differences were reported for two visual cues, they apparently were a function of statistical artifacts. A significant difference for the posture shifts cue was caused by the extreme results of a single study in the medium planning condition, and a significant difference for the pupil dilation cue occurred because there were no studies that measured this cue in the medium planning subgroup. In fact, the estimates for pupil dilation in the high and low planning subgroups were almost identical.

Two vocal cues, response latency and speech rate, were influenced by the level of planning. Deceivers in the high planning group displayed shorter response latencies and more rapid speech rates than deceivers in the low planning group.

The subgroup analyses highlight the difficulty researchers face when drawing conclusions about the role of nonverbal behavior in deception. Four cues influenced by motivation, gaze, head movements, posture shifts, and speech rate, and two cues influenced by planning, response latency and speech rate, did not correlate significantly with deception in the overall analysis.

In addition, these subgroup analyses emphasize the importance of the procedural issues addressed above. Though planning had little effect on the nonverbal correlates of deception, motivation appeared to be an important factor. Highly motivated deceivers behaved very differently from those with low motivation. This finding underscores the difficulty of discussing the role of nonverbal correlates of deception without first identifying important features of the deceptive situation.

VERBAL CORRELATES OF DECEPTION

Specific Cues

Since comparatively little research has been conducted on the verbal correlates of deception (Cody et al., 1984; Knapp et al., 1974; Stiff & Miller, 1986), it is impossible to make definite statements about these cues. Similarities among the findings of these studies, however, allow us to draw some interesting tentative conclusions, for there is considerable overlap in the specific cues studied.

The most consistent verbal correlate of deception is the number of words in a response. Deceptive statements are typically shorter than truthful ones. Given the cognitive effort required to develop and communicate deceptive responses, it makes sense that deceivers try to provide only requested information and to keep their responses brief. Unnecessary elaboration increases the opportunity for contradiction and the likelihood of detection.

Deceptive statements also tend to be more general and to contain fewer specific references about people, places, and temporal ordering of events. In addition, deceptive statements evidence considerable leveling, the tendency to overgeneralize using terms such as *all, every, none,* and *nobody.*

Less agreement exists regarding the role of self-interest statements and personal references in deceptive messages. Knapp et al. (1974) observed fewer self-experience statements, fewer self-references, and fewer self-interest statements in deceptive messages than in truthful ones. Stiff and Miller (1986), on the other hand, reported that deceptive statements contained more self-references and statements of personal responsibility than truthful utterances. This inconsistency suggests that differences in the contexts of deceptive interactions are likely to influence the verbal cues associated with truth and deception. Additional research is needed to identify verbal cues that signal deception across a variety of contexts and those cues that indicate deception in some contexts, but not in others.

General Assessments

Two studies (Kraut, 1978; Stiff & Miller, 1986) investigated general assessments of verbal content by asking raters to make a series of assessments about the plausibility, consistency, concreteness, and clarity of verbal responses. As noted earlier, because these four factors are usually highly intercorrelated, we collapsed them into a single variable labeled "verbal content."

Though Kraut (1978) reported that only plausibility was correlated with deception, we found that the composite measure of all four factors was also correlated. In fact, this composite measure was by far the strongest *verbal or nonverbal* correlate of deception ($r = .40$).

As stressed earlier, we endorse this holistic approach to studying verbal correlates of deception. Although investigation of specific verbal cues is important, we feel it is equally desirable to investigate the types of assessments individuals make during interaction. This is particularly true when one considers that individuals are unlikely to direct attention at several specific verbal cues during interactions.[2] It seems more plausible to assume that people consider the content of the conversation as a whole and make an overall assessment of a speaker's believability based on characteristics such as clarity, consistency, plausibility, and concreteness.

CORRELATES OF DECEPTIVE JUDGMENTS

Perhaps the most surprising aspect of our review of prior deception research lies in the relative lack of interest that has been shown in the verbal and nonverbal correlates of deceptive judgments. Many researchers have investigated either correlates of actual deception *or* correlates of deception detection accuracy, but few have integrated these two research traditions. However, our understanding of deceptive communication will not be complete until researchers examine the verbal and nonverbal correlates of *veracity judgments*. These correlates reflect the perceptions and stereotypes people have about deceptive behavior, and are a critical ingredient in our understanding of the deception detection process.

Although asking and answering such questions requires more effort than studies limited to either the correlates of deception or the level of detection accuracy, the payoffs justify the effort. For example, a study we conducted (Stiff & Miller, 1986) produced very surprising findings. Using the Exline procedure we interviewed students who either told the truth about their performance of a task or lied to cover up the fact that they had cheated. We videotaped the interviews and coded their verbal and nonverbal content. Following this step, we showed the interviews to another group of students at a different university and asked them to make judgments about the veracity of the person in each interview. We then correlated the judgments of veracity with the verbal and nonverbal content in each interview.

Our findings indicated that observers relied heavily on verbal and nonverbal cues to make judgments of veracity. Seven nonverbal cues: blinks, smiles, hand gestures, posture shifts, pauses, response duration, and response latency, and five verbal cues: statements of other responsibility, statements of mutual responsibility, mutual references, number of words, and general assessments of verbal content, were moderately or strongly correlated with *judgments* of veracity. However, none of the nonverbal cues and only two of the verbal cues, number of words and general assessments of verbal content, were moderately or strongly correlated with *actual* veracity.

These findings are consistent with at least three other studies (Kraut, 1978; Maier & Janzen, 1967; Riggio & Friedman, 1983) that examined a smaller number of cues. Although the number of investigations is limited, the findings are clear. The cues observers rely on to make judgments of veracity are, for the most part, unrelated to actual honesty and deceit.

Although these findings have received relatively little attention, we believe them to be among the most important outcomes of prior research on deception. The fact that people apparently use the "wrong" cues to make judgments of deceit underlies the inability to detect deception accurately and helps to explain why the success rate has been so low in most deception detection studies. At the same time this result highlights one possible avenue for future investigations of deception detection errors.

SUMMARY

Our view of the deception literature leads to several important conclusions about the role of verbal and nonverbal behavior in the deception process. First, though others may disagree, we believe it is time to move beyond the investigation of visual correlates of deception. Our review of the literature causes us to conclude that visual cues are not the most useful and reliable indicators of veracity. Instead, future studies should concentrate on verbal and vocal correlates of deception. Early attempts to unveil a "deception code" consisting of specific behavioral cues have proved unsuccessful. As a result, studies of behaviors associated with deception should seek to become more theoretically focused. The Cody et al. (1984) study offers an excellent example of the benefits of sound conceptual reasoning and reinforces our belief that it is time to move away from the variable-analytic paradigm that has dominated most prior deception research.

Finally, investigation of behavioral correlates of deception should be linked with the investigation of behavioral correlates of deceptive judgments. Preliminary work in this area has revealed a potential explanation for errors in deception detection. It is important to bear in mind that *judgments of veracity,* and not veracity itself, dictate many of the social and legal consequences typically associated with honesty and deceit. For example, in courtroom settings *perceptions* of witness veracity influence the legal disposition of the case. Given the social, economic, and relational weight associated with judgments of veracity, it is imperative that we gain a better understanding of factors that affect this judgment process.

NOTES

1. We adopted DeVito and Hecht's definition that *"nonverbal communication involves all messages 'other than words' including aspects of the voice, body movements, facial expressions, time, smell, and objects"* (1990, p. 5). This definition enables us to distinguish between visual and vocal nonverbal cues that are central to many investigations of deception.

Visual nonverbal cues consist of visually detectable bodily movements that often accompany verbal content; for example, indirect eye contact and unnecessary leg and foot movements. Vocal nonverbal cues consist of paralinguistic variables accompanying verbal content, for example, stuttering, long silent pauses, voice pitch, and speaking rate. Both visual and vocal cues may enhance, clarify, or contradict the semantic meaning of the verbal content.

Conversely, we will define *verbal communication* as *those characteristics of messages that assume a linguistic form, either written or spoken, that convey socially shared meaning and that represent the content of what is being said.* Verbal cues include references to specific people or situations, statements of responsibility, responsiveness to prior queries, and so forth.

2. The fact that our coders focus on a single cue and code cues individually underscores the difficulty people have attending to several specific cues simultaneously. If we asked coders to code multiple specific cues simultaneously, the reliability of these estimates would decrease considerably.

5

Misjudging Veracity: The Inaccuracy of Human Lie Detectors

In the previous chapter, we mentioned that while some researchers have attempted to isolate the behavioral correlates of deception, others have investigated the ability of individuals to detect deception accurately. In this chapter we review research investigating deception detection. We will first discuss the detection accuracy rates found in prior studies, and we will then offer two explanations for human errors in deception detection.

As used in the literature, the term *deception detection* is something of a misnomer. Typical procedures ask participants to judge the veracity of both truthful and deceptive behavior. For example, Stiff and Miller (1986) asked observers to evaluate 40 different interviews. In half of them, the interviewee was responding truthfully; in half, the interviewee was lying. Since most prior studies used similar procedures, observers typically attempt to detect both *truth* and *deception*, and researchers sometimes report separate truth and deception detection accuracy scores. More frequently, however, findings are reported as an average of these two scores, and are then labeled "detection accuracy." Often overlooked is the fact that such studies tell us as much about discerning truth as they do about detecting deception. Our point is not to quibble about prior research procedures, but rather to emphasize the importance of truth detection and to isolate its role in the deception process. To avoid confusion, we will use the term *detection accuracy* to refer to the combination of truth and deception accuracy scores, and we will reserve the term *deception detection* for instances where we refer only to scores for deceptive messages.

DETECTION ACCURACY

Three reviews have sought to answer questions about human ability to detect truth and deception accurately. In an early quantitative review, DePaulo, Zuckerman, and Rosenthal concluded, "on the basis of available evidence, it is clear that although humans are far from infallible in their efforts to diagnose lies, they are substantially better at the task than would result merely by chance" (1980, p. 130). Kraut (1980) took issue with this claim by reviewing studies reporting detection accuracy in percentage terms. He concluded, "accuracy scores rarely exceed 65% where 50% is chance level (M = 57.0%, SD = 7.8%)" (p. 209). Although studies included in these two reviews differ, their outcomes are more similar than suggested by their contradictory conclusions. Both reviews indicate that humans can detect deception at better than chance levels, but not much better. In a more thorough review, including both published and unpublished studies, Kalbfleisch (1985) found that cumulative accuracy ratings in prior research clustered from 45% to 70%. Rarely did accuracy scores depart from this range.

Indeed, two studies suggest that even professionals who are trained to detect deception have difficulty making accurate judgments. Kraut and Poe (1980) found that customs inspectors were equally inaccurate in their judgments of deception as laypeople. Recently, Ekman and O'Sullivan (1991) reported that several occupational groups, including federal polygraphers, robbery investigators, judges, and psychiatrists, were not significantly more accurate at detecting deception than college students. In their study, only secret service agents were more successful detectors than people in the other detection groups, but their accuracy rate was only 64%.

These findings lead us to conclude that humans are poor lie detectors. Although significant differences in detection accuracy have been observed across experimental conditions in some prior studies, overall detection accuracy scores rarely exceed chance probabilities, particularly in the majority of studies where communicators were lying and telling the truth with equal frequency. In general, people are only slightly more accurate than a flip of a coin when making judgments of truth and deception.

Although prior studies have generally yielded mediocre outcomes in detection accuracy, people consistently report extremely high levels of confidence in their detection ability. The implications of this finding are obvious: Even though people's actual success rate is low, their confidence in their judgments is high. For truthful communicators who are for some reason or other judged to be lying, this gap between actual accuracy and perceived confidence is discouraging; for the skillful liar, it is a heartening inconsistency. Perhaps the greatest danger in everyday interaction is the misplaced confidence persons have in their detection skills.

For the most part, researchers have been reluctant to conclude that people are not very good at detecting deception. The brief exchange in the literature between DePaulo et al. (1980) and Kraut (1980) illustrates this fact. Since then, however, few researchers have endorsed the position that humans are poor lie detectors.

We offer two possible explanations for the reluctance to assign individuals poor grades as deception detectors. First, many deception detection studies have been comparative; they were not intended to assess detection accuracy per se, but rather to identify differences in detection accuracy across two or more experimental conditions. In such studies, primary concern is directed at situational, relational, or personality factors that influence detection accuracy. Comparative analyses are conducted and results are presented in terms of differences in detection accuracy scores across conditions.

Two examples illustrate this point. In their classic study of deception detection, Ekman and Friesen (1974) asked observers to judge the veracity of nursing students who were instructed to lie or communicate truthfully about their reactions to pleasant and unpleasant film clips. Observers watched videotapes that depicted either the head-only or body-only of nursing students as they presented their messages. Though we question the utility of asking observers to make veracity judgments of a decapitated body, comparisons revealed significant differences in detection accuracy scores across conditions; observers viewing the body-only were generally more accurate than those viewing the head-only. However, detection accuracy scores exceeded chance probabilities in only one (body-only/deceptive messages—63.5%) of the eight experimental conditions. Unfortunately, the comparative analyses obscure the finding that overall detection accuracy was low (49.2%) and that even in the most accurate condition observers were far from perfect in their judgments.

A later study by Brandt, Miller, and Hocking (1982) manipulated exposure to truthful baseline information and assessed its influence on detection accuracy. They compared detection accuracy scores across groups with no exposure, one exposure, and two exposures to baseline information. Although significant differences in detection accuracy were observed across these three conditions, the highest level of accuracy was only 56% (two exposure condition). When compared to the no exposure condition (31%) this difference was sizeable; nevertheless, concern with the relative accuracy between groups tends to obscure the low absolute accuracy level among groups. Although we do not seek to criticize the research questions investigated in prior studies, we think it is important to point out that an emphasis on relative detection accuracy has led to an underemphasis on the importance of absolute detection accuracy.

A second possible explanation for the failure to stress findings that illustrate the relative inability to detect deception stems from the consequences of drawing this conclusion. For years researchers have been interested in identifying situational, relational, and personality factors that influence detection accuracy. Prior studies reveal that although these factors do influence detection accuracy, few, if any, produce accuracy rates exceeding 70%. Such a conclusion questions the importance of further deception detection research dealing with these factors. If overall accuracy rates are consistently low, perhaps it is time to declare deception detection a "dead area" or at least to alter radically our approaches to studying it.

We believe that the latter alternative is preferable to the former. In addition to investigating factors that facilitate or hinder deception detection, it would be useful to examine factors that produce errors in detection; that is, instead of investigating detection accuracy, researchers should begin to identify explanations for detection errors. In the next section we discuss two preliminary explanations for errors in veracity judgments.

EXPLANATIONS FOR DETECTION ERRORS

Two explanations for errors in truth and deception detection have dominated the literature. The first centers on information processing patterns of people who attempt to detect deception and the second focuses on the idiosyncratic nature of truthful and deceptive messages. Though neither explanation has been convincingly documented, both have received considerable attention by researchers.

Information Processing Errors

Thus far, we have arrived at two major conclusions about deceptive interactions. In Chapter 4, we concluded that the nonverbal cues individuals rely on to make judgments of veracity are, for the most part, unrelated to actual truth and deception. In this chapter, we argued that individuals are not very good at detecting deception. In combination, these conclusions highlight the importance of human information processing during deceptive transactions. It is likely that people's relative inability to detect deception results from a misplaced emphasis on informational cues that are poor indicators of veracity. In short, the information processing errors of intended deceivees may be responsible for detection errors.

The Distraction Hypothesis. Several information processing errors have been invoked as possible explanations for detection inaccuracy. The first of these was offered as a post hoc explanation for some rather unexpected findings in an early study by Maier and Thurber (1968). These researchers asked actors to role play a series of interviews in which an instructor was interrogating a student about a potential cheating incident. Research participants were exposed to differing presentations of the interviews and asked to rate the honesty of the student. In one condition participants watched the interviews live; in a second they listened to an audio recording of the interviews; and in a third they read transcripts of the interviews. Results indicated that participants who read or listened to the interviews were significantly more accurate at detecting deception (77% and 77.3%, respectively) than those who watched the live interviews (58%). Maier and Thurber (1968) speculated that participants in the live condition may have been distracted by visual cues that were not part of the audio and written conditions. They suggested that the visual cues may have limited the processing of verbal and vocal information thus restricting detection accuracy.

Distraction is a familiar concept to students of persuasion. Although there are several specific hypotheses to account for its effects, the message comprehension explanation is most relevant to deception researchers. According to this explanation, the presence of distractors limits message comprehension and reduces the persuasive impact of messages (Insko, Turnbull, & Yandell, 1974; Zimbardo, Snyder, Thomas, Gold, & Gurwitz, 1970).

While Maier and Thurber (1968) never pursued a formal test of their distraction explanation, others did and it soon became one explanation for detection errors. Two studies (Bauchner et al., 1977; Hocking et al., 1979) provided further elaboration and tests of the hypothesis. While the Hocking et al. results generally supported the hypothesis, Bauchner et al. relied on procedural differences to resolve the inconsistencies between their findings and those of the prior two studies. Because of these studies of modality influences on detection accuracy, the distraction hypothesis gained acceptance as a plausible explanation for errors in truth and deception detection.

Unfortunately, these studies suffered from methodological flaws that prevented an adequate test of the distraction hypothesis. In all three studies the mode of message presentation was confounded with the type of cue information provided in the message. For example, Bauchner et al. (1977) exposed participants to audio-visual, audio-only, or transcript presentations of truthful and deceptive messages. Persons in the audio-visual condition were exposed to verbal, vocal, and visual cues; those in the audio-only condition were exposed to verbal and vocal cues; while those in the transcript condition were exposed to only verbal cues. This confound made it impossible to separate the influences of communication modality and type of cue information on detection errors, and thus prevented a fair test of the distraction hypothesis.

There are several theoretical reasons to expect that the mode of presenting information will influence judgments of honesty and deceit. For example, Wright (1981) found that people reported 25% more thoughts and twice as many supportive arguments or source derogations when an advertisement was presented in a written rather than an audio format. Such findings are consistent with Taylor and Thompson's conclusion that "those who have printed messages have the opportunity to go back to sections that were unclear, whereas the same opportunity is not afforded by T.V. or orally presented messages" (1982, p. 185). Indeed, Maier and Thurber alluded to this problem when they noted that "readers have the opportunity to re-read any section and hence can correct for losses of attention" (1968, p. 30).

In addition, it is likely that visual presentations are more vivid (Nisbett & Ross, 1980; Taylor & Thompson, 1982) and that they increase the salience of communicator-related information (Chaiken & Eagly, 1983). In fact, a recent study found that information vividness influenced perceptions of persuasiveness (Collins, Taylor, Wood, & Thompson, 1988). Taken together, the preceding two lines of research furnish strong evidence that the confound between the type of cue information and the mode of presentation prevented an adequate test of the distraction hypothesis.

This criticism highlights a dilemma for researchers investigating deceptive transactions: In real-world situations the availability of certain cues is determined by presentational mode. As a result, researchers seeking to capture realistic aspects of deceptive transactions may have to accept this confound as inevitable. Though a more elegant test of the distraction hypothesis involves separating the presentational mode and cue availability, such a procedure may be irrelevant to the issue of cue availability in many deceptive transactions. Recognizing this dilemma, we argued that a fair test of the distraction hypothesis required manipulation of verbal, vocal, and visual information without also varying the presentational mode (Stiff et al., 1989), thus permitting assessment of the influences of verbal and nonverbal information independent of the mode of presentation. To accomplish this objective, we asked actors to display truthful or deceptive verbal, visual, and vocal cues as they responded to an interviewer's questions. Verbal content was manipulated by having the actors provide either truthful (i.e., clear, consistent, plausible) or deceptive (i.e., vague, inconsistent, implausible) responses to the interviewer's questions. Truthful and deceptive visual content were manipulated by having the actors display varying amounts of three visual cues associated with deception (adaptors, eye gaze, and posture shifts), while truthful and deceptive vocal content were manipulated by varying the amount of three vocal cues (speech errors, audible pauses, and silent pauses) associated with deception.

We next showed these videotaped interviews to observers who were asked not only to make judgments of veracity but also to evaluate characteristics of verbal content in each of the interviews. If the distraction hypothesis is correct, the study should have produced two related findings: (1) Observers exposed to visual, vocal, and verbal cues should have relied primarily on visual cues to make judgments of veracity, and (2) the presence and type of visual cue information should have *distracted* observers from processing verbal content.

Results of our study did not support the distraction hypothesis. As in prior studies, observers relied heavily on nonverbal information to make judgments of veracity, but the presence or amount of nonverbal information did not prevent observers from processing verbal content. Observers were able to identify accurately features of the verbal content, a finding at odds with the distraction hypothesis. If the presence of visual cues were distracting, it would have prevented observers from identifying features of truthful and deceptive verbal content. In fact, the nonverbal cue manipulation exerted no effect on judgments of verbal content.

Since our findings provided no support for the distraction hypothesis, we were left to ask why observers relied almost exclusively on nonverbal cues to make judgments of veracity even though they could accurately identify truthful and deceptive verbal content. We eventually proposed a second information processing hypothesis to explain the importance attached to nonverbal cues when making veracity judgments, the situational familiarity hypothesis.

The Situational Familiarity Hypothesis. The situational familiarity hypothesis posits that observers faced with unfamiliar situations rely primarily on nonverbal cues to make veracity judgments because they have little or no basis for assessing the truthfulness of verbal content. In other words, when forced to decide, people in unfamiliar situations rely on cultural norms specifying what a liar "looks like" because these norms are more informative than the communicator's verbal responses. Although verbal cues may validly signal deceit, people unfamiliar with the factual circumstances are largely unable to assess the utility of these cues for detecting deception. Conversely, in familiar situations people are better able to "visualize" the events in question and to judge the believability of verbal content. Thus, people in familiar situations will rely primarily on verbal content to make veracity judgments (Stiff et al., 1989, p. 560).

The grounds for this hypothesis reside in literature on social cognition. Observers making attributions of truth and deception fall prey to a number of cognitive biases and heuristics (Kahneman, Slovic, & Tversky, 1982). Because people tend to be cognitive misers (Taylor, 1981; Taylor & Fiske, 1978; Wyer & Srull, 1981), they often rely on simple decision rules (heuristics) to make judgments of veracity. These simple decision rules often substitute for careful thinking about an issue. For example, people may possess a heuristic that "nervous behavior" is probably deceptive behavior. If they use this heuristic to evaluate nervous behavior, they may judge the source of the behavior as deceptive, without careful consideration of the remainder to the source's behavior.

Chaiken (1987) argued that the use of simple decision rules replaces systematic processing primarily when observers lack ability or motivation to scrutinize verbal content. Applying Chaiken's analysis, we reasoned that when messages are systematically processed, verbal content cues will exert the major influence on veracity judgments. Conversely, when people rely on heuristics, nonverbal cues will exert the most influence on veracity judgments.

The important distinction between the distraction and situational familiarity hypotheses lies in people's abilities to process verbal content presented in combination with nonverbal behaviors. The distraction hypothesis posits that the presence of visual cues prevents observers from processing verbal content. Conversely, the situational familiarity hypothesis posits that observers can process visual, vocal, and verbal cues simultaneously. The importance that observers assign to these cues depends on the extent to which they are familiar with the situation in question.

To test our hypothesis, we showed videotaped interviews to observers. The actress in these interviews displayed either truthful or deceptive visual cues while responding to an interviewer's questions using either truthful or deceptive verbal statements. In addition, we varied the situation described in the interviews. In half of them, a police detective was questioning a college student about a recent auto accident that occurred locally. The street names and buildings described in the interview were all familiar to the study participants. In the remaining interviews, the accident was situated in a distant city. Participants in the study indicated they were unfamiliar with the location of buildings or streets depicted in these interviews.

We hypothesized that participants exposed to the familiar context would rely primarily on verbal content to make judgments of veracity while those exposed to the unfamiliar situations would rely primarily on visual cues. Our findings were only partially supportive of our original hypotheses. As expected, observers of the familiar situation relied almost exclusively on verbal content cues to make veracity judgments. Contrary to our expectation, however, those exposed to the unfamiliar situation relied on both verbal and visual cues to make judgments. Thus, our study provided partial support for the hypothesis that people rely more on heuristics (e.g., visual cues) in unfamiliar situations than in familiar ones. This conclusion coincides with the reasoning of prior researchers who argue that the relative importance of verbal and nonverbal information is determined by situational factors (Krauss, Apple, Morency, Wenzel, & Winton, 1981; Zuckerman, Amidon, Bishop, & Pomerantz, 1982).

These findings suggest several important theoretical and practical implications. Theoretically, they support an alternative explanation for the primacy of nonverbal cues in prior deception studies. Observed differences in the relative reliance on visual cues in familiar and unfamiliar situations suggest that caution be exercised when generalizing the findings of prior deception studies to everyday deceptive interactions. Because the lion's share of prior deception research has used situations unfamiliar to research participants, the primacy of nonverbal cues in these studies may well have occurred because of the nature of the experimental situation. If so, the findings may not be representative of deceptive judgments in natural interactions where participants are familiar with the situation. Indeed, the most consistent finding in deception research may be just an artifact of the procedures typically used in prior studies and not a reflection of people's preferences for nonverbal information.

We are not suggesting, of course, that natural deceptive situations are always familiar to participants. Situational familiarity varies from interaction to interaction, and people encounter various unfamiliar situations every day. What we are stressing, however, is the potential role of situational familiarity in the processing of verbal and nonverbal cues to arrive at judgments of veracity.

Although preliminary, our findings have implications for a wide variety of political, social, and legal contexts. In a legal context, for example, reliance on verbal and nonverbal sources of information may depend on the extent to which lawyers can sufficiently familiarize jurors with contextual features of witness testimony. Jurors who are relatively unfamiliar with the context in which testimony is situated may rely on a variety of information sources to make sense of the proceedings. On the other hand, jurors who are relatively familiar with the situation may feel confident relying primarily on verbal cues to make assessments of witness veracity.

In summary, the distraction hypothesis provides a questionable information processing explanation for judgmental errors. By contrast, the situational familiarity hypothesis remains a viable potential explanation for errors in veracity judgments, although further research of this explanation is needed.

If, as we have speculated, situational familiarity has influenced detection accuracy in prior research, the generalizability of detection accuracy scores produced in these earlier studies is open to serious question. In turn, such a conclusion implies that prior research has underestimated the ability of individuals to judge the veracity of others. Yet another alternative explanation for low detection accuracy scores stresses the individual nature of deceptive interactions. Perhaps deceptive communication is highly individualistic, and not subject to simple generalizations. If so, then low detection accuracy scores may simply indicate the complexity of deceptive interactions. In the next section we discuss this alternative explanation and examine findings that are consistent with it.

Idiosyncratic Behaviors

The possibility that much deceptive behavior is idiosyncratic is worthy of consideration. Although generalizations about verbal and nonverbal correlates of truth and deception summarized in Chapter 4 are inconsistent with this assertion, these behaviors constitute an incomplete description of truthful and deceptive behavior. While some characteristics of truthful and deceptive behavior are probably shared by many people, most individuals manifest specific communicative nuances that distinguish them from others. To the extent that such nuances exist and contribute to an individual's "communicative style," attempts to judge veracity without prior knowledge of a communicator's idiosyncracies are unlikely to be successful.

The value of knowledge about idiosyncratic behavior is underscored by Miller et al. (1986), who argued that the availability of truthful baseline information may be an important determinant of deception detection accuracy. Armed with extensive knowledge of another's truthful behavior, deception detection becomes easier. Deviations from typical communicative behaviors signal the possibility of deception and warrant closer scrutiny of the situation. In other words, baseline information affords detectors the opportunity to compare potentially suspicious behaviors with those known to represent truthful communication. The importance of baseline information is dependent on the extent to which such comparisons facilitate deception detection.

Three studies investigated the influence of truthful baseline information on deception detection accuracy (Brandt et al., 1980a, 1980b, 1982). In the first study, these researchers manipulated familiarity with baseline information by varying the number of times observers viewed a truthful interview. In the no baseline information condition, observers were not exposed to the truthful interview. In the low, moderate, and high conditions observers were exposed to the same truthful interview once, three times, and six times respectively. Following this induction, observers were exposed to the critical interview and asked to judge the veracity of the interviewee. By using several stimulus people, the researchers were able to vary the veracity of interviewees during the critical interview.

Findings indicated that familiarity with truthful baseline information influenced judgmental accuracy. In the no baseline information condition, detection accuracy was only 38%. Accuracy increased in the low (51%) and moderate (59%) baseline information conditions before falling to 44% in the high baseline information condition. Brandt et al.

(1980a) offered two potential explanations for the low accuracy scores in the high exposure condition: Observers may have experienced information overload that could have caused a perceptual distortion of baseline information, or observers may have become fatigued or bored with the experimental task. The boredom explanation is most appealing because the familiarity manipulation consisted of several exposures to a small segment of a communicator's truthful behavior. Brandt et al. hypothesized that after three exposures to the same information, additional exposures provided little new information and may have inhibited detection accuracy. Detection inaccuracy in the high baseline familiarity condition notwithstanding, the overall findings support the position that familiarity with the idiosyncratic behaviors of another facilitated judgmental accuracy.

Two additional studies produced similar findings. Brandt et al. (1980b) found that observers who watched truthful baseline information three times were more accurate (66%) than those who received no baseline information (42%). A third study (Brandt et al., 1982) revealed that observers exposed to the baseline information once or twice were more accurate (52% and 56%) at detecting deception than those who received no baseline information.

Zuckerman, Koestner, and Alton (1984) used a different procedure to study the effect of baseline information on judgmental accuracy. These researchers asked observers to make a series of judgments about a communicator's veracity. They manipulated baseline information by varying the number of times observers received feedback about the communicator's truthfulness (zero, four, or eight times) and by varying when this information was provided (before or after exposure to the interview segment). Zuckerman et al. found that the more information observers received about the communicator's actual veracity, the more accurate they judged subsequent interview segments. Consistent with the notion of an idiosyncratic deception code, Zuckerman et al. also found that feedback about a particular communicator was not helpful in judging the veracity of other communicators.

These results underscore the importance of idiosyncratic behavior in deception. In each study observers privy to baseline information about a communicator were better able to detect deception than those with no baseline information. Furthermore, with one exception, the more baseline information observers received, the greater their accuracy. Although it is impossible to assess the percentage of communicative behavior that is subject to generalizations and the percentage that is

idiosyncratic, knowledge about a person's unique communicative characteristics permitted observers in these studies to identify deviations from
typical communicative patterns when making judgments of veracity.

A natural extension of this research would be to investigate the
influence of relational development on detection accuracy. Even though
people in well-developed relationships probably have considerably
more baseline information about their partners than persons in less
developed relationships, relational development also influences a number of additional factors (e.g., a truth bias) that are likely to inhibit
deception detection (discussed in Chapter 6). In this regard, the procedures used by Brandt et al. (1980a, 1980b, 1982) and Zuckerman et al.
(1984) can be used effectively to isolate the influence of baseline
information without introducing the relational baggage common to
well-developed personal relationships.

Thus, it appears that without knowledge of person-specific communicative features it is often difficult to detect deception accurately. When
observers are provided with baseline information about a message source,
their ability to judge the source's veracity improves considerably. In
general, the more baseline information people have, the more accurate
they become (Kalbfleisch, 1985; Zuckerman et al., 1984).

These findings provide a second explanation for the low detection
accuracy scores observed in prior research. Strangers with no knowledge about a target's idiosyncracies are less able to separate truthful
and deceptive messages. Relational partners apparently fare no better
at detecting deception. Although they may possess the baseline information necessary for such judgments, as we shall discuss in Chapter 6,
additional relational factors are likely to inhibit their suspicion and
result in detection errors.

A third explanation for low detection accuracy awaits empirical
investigation. It is possible that higher detection rates are socially
dysfunctional: People who are adept at detecting deception may learn
unpleasant things about themselves and others that they would rather
not know. Because some deceptive messages are pro-social in nature
(white lies and insincere compliments) and others are painful to detect
(relational transgressions), it is possible that targets may sometimes
actively avoid detecting deception. That is, people may "learn" how to
avoid the truth. Though untested, we tentatively offer this explanation
as a possibility and a direction for future research.

SUMMARY AND CONCLUSIONS

Perhaps the clearest conclusion emerging from our review of this literature is that humans are relatively poor lie detectors. Although researchers in this field have been somewhat reluctant to reach this conclusion, prior research findings clearly point to it. Two explanations for human inability to discriminate between truthful and deceptive messages have been discussed. Investigation of human information processing patterns is one avenue for further research on detection accuracy. As predicted, our own findings were inconsistent with the distraction hypothesis, but they did establish the potential role of situational familiarity in the deception process. Furthermore, these findings pose questions about the generalizability of prior studies that have placed detectors in unfamiliar situations.

The second explanation for detection errors holds that deceptive behavior is highly idiosyncratic. Though this explanation is at odds with research on behavioral correlates of deception (discussed in Chapter 4), its possible merit implies a pessimistic outlook for researchers attempting to inventory generalizations about deceptive transactions. Perhaps one solution to this apparent contradiction lies in the speculation that the deception code contains some elements that are easily discernible and highly generalizable and others that are more subtle and idiosyncratic (Zuckerman ct al., 1984, p. 526).

6

Factors Influencing the Judgments of Veracity

In Chapter 5 we argued that people have difficulty detecting deception when it occurs. Although detection accuracy rates in prior investigations rarely exceeded 60%, there is considerable variance in accuracy scores across situations. Deception is more easily detected in some situations than in others. Research has attempted to identify situational features that influence a target's ability to recognize deception when it occurs. In this chapter we will review the findings of these investigations and discuss the importance of situational constraints in the deception detection process.

Four situational factors have received prominent attention in prior research on deception detection. We begin our review with a discussion of the influence of *emotional and factual content* on detection accuracy. People often devise deceptive messages to conceal their true emotions about a person or issue. In other situations the deception involves misrepresentation of factual information. Our review of situational factors begins with a discussion of the effect of message content on detection accuracy. *Planning* is a second situational factor that affects deception detection accuracy. Some deceptive transactions require spontaneous preparation of deceptive messages, while others permit deceivers to plan and rehearse their statements carefully. We review the influence of planning and rehearsal on deception detection accuracy. *Interrogative probes* are a third characteristic of some deceptive transactions. In these transactions, sources interact with targets of deception who are afforded the opportunity to ask questions and challenge the responses of a deceiver. In other situations, deceptive messages are presented in a linear fashion leaving little opportunity to challenge a source's veracity. We finish the chapter with an in-depth discussion of the effects of *relational development* on both deception and deception detection. While many deceptive transactions involve relative strangers, deceptive situations frequently arise among relational partners as well. Recent investigations have isolated important differences in the detection processes of strangers and relational partners. These findings are included in our review of situational characteristics of deceptive transactions.

DETECTING EMOTIONAL AND FACTUAL DECEPTION

One issue that has received attention in the deception literature is the influence of message content on deception and detection accuracy. If asked to recall a recent deceptive episode, most people are likely to recall a situation in which the factual content of a message was inaccurate or misleading. Though factual deception is a common occurrence, people often attempt to deceive one another about their emotions as well. Relational partners often feel compelled to refrain from providing honest assessments of their feelings about sensitive relational issues. For example, in the early stages of relational development couples may hide their true emotions because they are uncertain about the effects of honesty on the relationship.

While deception about factual information has been the focus of extensive research, relatively few studies have investigated deception about emotional reactions to people and situations. Ekman and Friesen's (1974) early research on deceptive communication and the "leakage hypothesis" was the first to address this aspect of the deception process. Recall that Ekman and Friesen asked nursing students to view either pleasant or unpleasant pictures and describe their *emotional* reactions to them. Although they experimentally confounded the emotional content of the pictures with the truth and deception manipulation (nurses viewing the pleasant pictures were truthful while those viewing unpleasant pictures were deceptive), the study was instrumental in drawing attention to the distinction between emotional and factual deception.

Hocking et al. (1979) compared factual and emotional deception across a wide variety of presentational modes. People in their study were asked to behave truthfully and deceptively about both factual and emotional content. Findings indicated that observers were more accurate when judging the veracity of factual statements (54%) than they were when judging the veracity of emotional statements (50%). Participants in this study were strangers, and it is questionable whether findings would hold for people in interpersonal relationships. The strangers in this study may have lacked the background information about the source's "typical" emotional disposition necessary for highly accurate judgments about emotional statements. Partners in developed relationships, on the other hand, may possess sufficient baseline information to more accurately identify deviations from typical emotional states. While this issue is more centrally related to relational deception, further research is warranted to identify the relative accuracy of targets attempting to detect these two forms of deception.

Unfortunately, research has yet to investigate differences in nonverbal behaviors associated with factual and emotional deception. In Chapter 4 we discussed two different theoretical explanations for the presence of nonverbal behavior during deception. The cognitive perspective argues that deception requires more cognitive effort, while arousal explanations suggest that the costs associated with detection produce heightened physiological arousal in deceivers. Perhaps both explanations are correct, each applying to a separate domain. For example, it may be that emotional deception heightens a deceiver's arousal, while factual deception is more closely associated with the cognitive effort necessary to deceive effectively. If this is the case, one might expect different nonverbal cues to be associated with the two forms of deception. For example, cues associated with arousal (posture shifts, adaptors, speech errors) should be more prevalent in emotional deceptions than in factual deceptions. Conversely, cues associated with cognitive effort (response latencies, pauses, pupil dilation) should be more prevalent in factual than in emotional deceptions. Once again, however, these questions await further investigation.

DETECTING PLANNED AND SPONTANEOUS DECEPTION

Deception is often a carefully planned communicative strategy. Knowledge about people and situations permit interactants to anticipate interactions in which deception is viewed as a favorable alternative to the truth. Dating partners anticipate inquires about their behavior in prior relationships and consider the consequences of revealing the "whole truth." In legal settings, witnesses rehearse testimony prior to courtroom appearances. Prior to a screening interview job applicants carefully consider how best to explain negative features of their employment record.

While these situations and others like them allow interactants to plan and rehearse a deceptive message, other deceptive transactions call for more spontaneous message production. A child who has been caught stealing a candy bar may not have anticipated being caught, and hence may not have considered how best to account for his or her behavior. An employee who calls in sick in order to attend an afternoon baseball game may not anticipate encountering a supervisor while at the ballpark. If deception is to be successfully perpetrated in situations like these, deceivers must not only attempt to control verbal and nonverbal clues to deception, they must also control verbal and nonverbal behaviors associated with the surprise of the situation.

Initial investigations of this issue focused exclusively on the verbal and nonverbal cues associated with planned and spontaneous deceptive messages (Matarazzo, Wiens, Jackson, & Manaugh, 1970; O'Hair, Cody, & McLaughlin, 1981; see Chapter 4 for a discussion of these effects). One of the first studies to investigate the effects of planning on *detection accuracy* was conducted by Littlepage and Pineault (1982). They found that observers more accurately detected spontaneous than planned deceptive messages. Interestingly, there were no differences in the judgments of planned and spontaneous truthful messages.

Recently, three explanations have been proposed to account for the effect of planning on detection accuracy. The first explanation holds that when given the opportunity to plan their deception, deceivers will experience less *arousal* and exhibit fewer nonverbal cues typically associated with deception. The second explanation posits that the opportunity to plan deceptive messages reduces the *cognitive effort* required to produce them and reduces the number of accompanying nonverbal behaviors associated with deception. The third explanation argues that planning and rehearsal benefit some deceivers and are a detriment to others. According to this explanation, a person's level of *self-monitoring* determines whether he or she is likely to benefit from planning and rehearsal. Each of these explanations is explored below.

Planning and Arousal

Differences in the physiological arousal of truthful and deceptive communicators may provide the key to understanding these findings. The opportunity to plan and rehearse a deceptive message may serve to decrease the level of arousal typically associated with deception (Chapter 4). If this occurs, then one would expect differences in the behaviors associated with planned and spontaneous deceptive messages. Because truthful messages are less physiologically arousing, planning and rehearsal should have limited influence on the production of truthful messages.

To test this explanation, DePaulo, Lanier, and Davis (1981) investigated differences in observer accuracy when judging planned and spontaneous messages and found no differences in the judgments of planned and spontaneous deceptive messages. Using self-reports and observer ratings, they also found no differences in the level of arousal between deceivers who were given the opportunity to plan their message and those who deceived spontaneously.

Planning and Cognition

In the midst of these conflicting findings, two related studies (Cody, Marston, & Foster, 1984; Greene, O'Hair, Cody, & Yen, 1985) offered a different theoretical explanation for the effects of planning on deception. Their thinking coincided with research in interpersonal communication that emphasized the importance of cognition in the planning and execution of communicative goals (Berger, 1988; Dillard, 1990; Greene, 1984). Greene et al. (1985) argued that deceptive messages required more cognitive effort to plan than truthful ones: Deceivers are not only concerned with developing a convincing message, they must also be cautious not to contradict prior statements or the knowledge of message targets. They further argued that the cognitive effort required to produce deceptive messages is evidenced by specific nonverbal behaviors associated with cognitive processing (e.g., response latency).

Consistent with this rationale, Cody et al. (1984) and Greene et al. (1985) argued that planning should decrease the cognitive load required for deceptive message production and hypothesized that planned lies would contain fewer response latencies than spontaneous ones. Although the findings of these two studies were consistent with this hypothesis, neither study investigated the relationship between planned and spontaneous lies and *detection accuracy*. Thus, while these studies offer another theoretical reason to expect that planned lies will be more difficult to detect than spontaneous ones, they provide no information about the influence of planning on deception detection.

While the arousal and cognitive-load explanations for planning effects seem straightforward, investigations of these hypotheses produced a number of contradictory findings. Findings from the DePaulo et al. (1980) study were inconsistent with Littlepage and Pineault (1982) findings, providing a confusing account of the influence of planning on arousal.

The Cody et al. (1984) and Greene et al. (1985) studies provided some support for the hypothesized role of cognition in planned and spontaneous deception; however, both of these studies produced findings that were inconsistent with subsidiary hypotheses about the effects of cognition. Though it may be intuitively obvious that the opportunity to plan a deceptive message increases its effectiveness, scientific evidence for this conclusion is scarce.

Self-Monitoring and Planned Deception

One possibility for resolving these apparently inconsistent findings may be to consider the role of personality in the deception process. One personality factor that has been demonstrated to influence social interaction is *self-monitoring.*

Since its inception, the self-monitoring construct has been used in a variety of research programs to account for individual differences in interaction style. Snyder (1974), who first developed the self-monitoring construct, and other scholars (Lennox & Wolfe, 1984) have contributed to the conceptual definition and measurement of this construct.

Self-monitoring is a personality factor that assesses a person's tendency to monitor and respond to external cues in social interactions. High self-monitors are social chameleons, capable of adapting their interaction style to the constraints of particular interactions. High self-monitors are adept at interpreting and responding to social cues and are highly concerned with maintaining socially appropriate behavior. Conversely, low self-monitors exhibit a constant interaction style, rarely adapting their behavior to meet the social constraints of an interaction. Compared to high self-monitors, they are inattentive to social cues and unconcerned with the social appropriateness of their behavior.

The first investigation of self-monitoring and planned deception emphasized the role of information acquisition in the planning process. Elliott (1979) asked high and low self-monitors to convey a truthful or fabricated impression of themselves while interacting with others. Interactants were given time to plan their self-presentations and provided the opportunity to "acquire" information about the other interactants. Interactants were paid $2.50 for participating in the study and allowed to spend up to 15 cents of that money to purchase biographical, attitudinal, or personality information about the other interactants.

Because high self-monitors are guided by external social cues, Elliott argued they would purchase more information about the other interactants than low self-monitors, who were likely to be guided by their own internal beliefs about how best to convey the intended impression. Consistent with this hypothesis, results indicated that high self-monitors bought more total information than low self-monitors when planning both truthful and fabricated impressions. In addition, high self-monitors purchased more biographical and attitudinal information about others when preparing fabricated as opposed to truthful impressions.

These findings suggest that people may differ in their cognitive approaches to planning truthful and deceptive messages. High self-monitors were eager to acquire information about the targets of their messages while low self-monitors were content to be guided by their own internal beliefs about the interaction. Unfortunately, this study provides little information about the influence of differential planning on the production and success of truthful and deceptive messages.

The role of self-monitoring in the planning and execution of truthful and deceptive messages was explored by Miller, deTurck, and Kalbfleisch (1983). Combining prior findings on self-monitoring and arousal, they argued that while high self-monitors should benefit from planning and rehearsal, this opportunity would be counterproductive for low self-monitors. Miller et al. argued that low self-monitors may realize they are ineffective deceivers and be less likely to plan and rehearse deceptive messages. Hence, any time allocated for planning and rehearsal serves only to heighten the arousal of low self-monitors and further detracts from their ability to produce a convincing message.

Consistent with their hypothesis, Miller et al. (1983) found that high self-monitors were more successful perpetrators of deception than low self-monitors and that this difference was most pronounced for deceivers who were given the opportunity to plan and rehearse their messages (Figure 6.1). Planning and rehearsal increased the effectiveness of high self-monitors but it was a detriment to the effectiveness of low self-monitors.

Analysis of deceivers' nonverbal behaviors provided a partial explanation for the differences in detection accuracy. Compared with rehearsed high self-monitors, unrehearsed low self-monitors displayed greater frequencies of pausing and nonfluency, and observers were more accurate at detecting deception perpetrated by unrehearsed low self-monitors (Miller et al., 1983, p. 113). While the size of these effects is not overwhelming, the pattern they produce is clear: Planning and rehearsal time are advantageous for high self-monitors and disadvantageous for low self-monitors.

These studies reflect the importance of planning and rehearsal in the deception process. While additional investigations are warranted, some

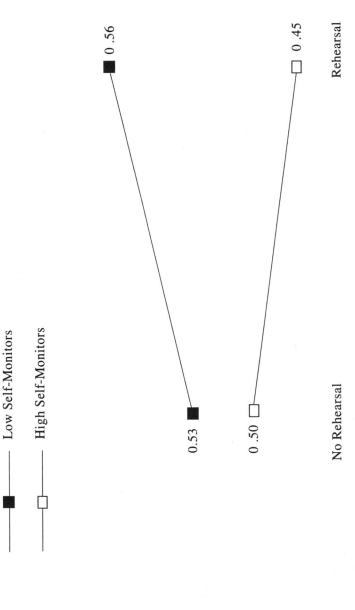

Figure 6.1. Accuracy of Detecting Deception Perpetrated by High and Low Self-Monitors
SOURCE: From "Self-Monitoring, Rehearsal, and Deceptive Communication," by G. R. Miller, M. A. deTurck, & P. J. Kalbfleisch, 1983, *Human Communication Research, 10*, pp. 97-117. Used by permission.

tentative generalizations can be advanced. First, planning appears to reduce the cognitive load necessary to produce a deceptive message. When given the opportunity to plan a message, deceivers exhibit fewer of the nonverbal cues associated with cognitive effort and fewer cues that indicate deception. The relationship between planning and arousal, however, is somewhat more complex. High self-monitors appear to use planning and rehearsal time to their advantage by seeking external information about the social setting. They also produce deceptive messages that are difficult to detect, partially because they contain fewer nonverbal behaviors that are typically associated with deception. Low self-monitors, on the other hand, do not use planning and rehearsal time to their advantage. They seek out little external information and produce deceptive messages that contain more nonverbal clues to deceit. Though preliminary, these generalizations suggest that the opportunity to plan is an important feature in deceptive interactions.

USING INTERROGATIVE PROBES TO DETECT DECEPTION

Another situational factor that influences veracity judgments and detection accuracy is the nature and extent of interrogative probes. As we mentioned in Chapter 3, much of the existing research has relied on a linear model for investigating deceptive communication. Most studies expose observers to a single message presentation and ask them to judge the source's veracity. While these research procedures may be consistent with the constraints of some deceptive situations (e.g., deception perpetrated through the mass media), deception in interpersonal contexts rarely involves these limitations.

In most interpersonal situations the process begins with a deceptive message that may or may not be effective. If the original statement is convincing, the deceptive attempt may be complete. If it is unconvincing, the target(s) of the deceptive message may ask additional questions and probe the source until the source is sufficiently persuasive or the deception is discovered. Responses to interrogative probes may provide additional verbal and nonverbal information that is not present in initial deceptive statements. Responses to probes require deceivers to clarify and expand the content of their prior statements. In addition to providing more information, these responses give targets the opportunity to compare statements and identify inconsistencies and ambiguities, two features of verbal content that influence veracity judgments.

In an initial attempt to investigate the influence of interrogative probes, Stiff and Miller (1986) manipulated both the intensity and direction of questions asked by targets of deception. Using a version of the Exline procedure (see Chapter 3 for details), participants were interviewed about their performance on a series of perceptual dot estimation exercises. Half of the participants were communicating truthfully about their performance, while the remaining participants communicated deceptively. Half of the truthful and deceptive communicators received "positive probes" from the interviewer while half received "negative probes." The positive probes were designed to convey that the interviewer believed the communicator's prior statement, but sought additional information. The negative probes also requested additional information, but conveyed a degree of skepticism about the communicator's prior statements.

Analysis of the responses associated with the probing manipulation revealed that, independent of actual honesty and deceit, the type of interrogative probes asked by the interviewer influenced the verbal and nonverbal behaviors of sources (Table 6.1). Sources receiving negative probes displayed fewer blinks ($r = -.33$) and more hand gestures ($r = .33$), smiled less ($r = -.24$), and had longer responses ($r = .20$) but shorter response latencies ($r = -.26$) than sources receiving positive probes. In addition, negative probes resulted in statements that contained more modifiers ($r = .33$) and statements of personal responsibility ($r = .20$), and fewer statements of other responsibility ($r = -.20$); more self-references ($r = .23$) and fewer mutual ($r = -.20$) and other-references ($r = -.21$) than positive probes (Stiff & Miller, 1986, p. 352).

In addition to their influence on the verbal and nonverbal behaviors of sources, interrogative probes also influenced observer judgments of honesty and deceit. Videotapes of these interviews were edited to remove the positive and negative probes and replace them with neutral probes. Observers viewing the edited videotapes judged sources who received negative probes as significantly more truthful than those who received positive probes. Because the positive and negative probes had been removed from these videotapes, it is unlikely that observers were influenced by the valence of the interviewer's questions. Instead, we argued that sources receiving negative probes may have realized that the deceptive attempt was in jeopardy and adapted their behavior accordingly. Research by Silverman, Rivera, and Tedeschi (1979) found that when people receive feedback indicating that others are suspicious about the validity of their statements, they modify their behavior to

TABLE 6.1

Correlations Between Visual, Vocal, and Verbal Cues and Message Veracity,
Probe Valence, and Judgments of Veracity

Cue	Message Veracity	Probe Valence	Veracity Judgment
Blinks	.10	−.33	.27
Smiles	.12	−.24	.46
Adaptors	−.19	−.17	.18
Hand gestures	.07	.33	−.32
Foot gestures	−.18	−.06	.16
Posture shifts	.04	.03	.40
Speech errors	.00	−.10	.09
Pauses	.03	.19	.60
Response duration	−.13	.20	−.37
Response latency	.15	−.26	.21
Statements of personal responsibility	.21	.20	.08
Statements of other responsibility	.10	−.20	.34
Statements of mutual responsibility	.05	.10	.31
Self-references	.22	.23	.05
Other-references	−.02	−.21	.17
Mutual references	−.05	−.20	.40
Modifiers	−.05	.33	−.03
Words	−.21	.12	−.42
Verbal content (e.g., consistency and plausibility)	−.40	.04	−.36

SOURCE: From "'Come to think to think of It' . . . : Interrogative Probes, Deceptive Communication, and Deception Detection," by J. B. Stiff & G. R. Miller, 1986, *Human Communication Research, 12*, pp. 339-357. Used by permission.
NOTE: Positive correlations reflect a positive relationship between the presence of the cues and either actual deceptiveness, negative probes, or perceived deceptiveness ($N = 40$).

become convincing. In our study, the verbal and nonverbal behaviors associated with the negative probes were also related to judgments of truthfulness. That is, people receiving negative probes displayed *more* of the behaviors that observers relied on to make judgments of honesty.

A recent replication of this investigation found support for these general findings (Buller, Strzyzewski, & Comstock, 1991). People who received probes indicating the target was suspicious altered their nonverbal behaviors in subsequent responses. Together, these studies (Buller et al., 1991; Stiff & Miller, 1986) indicate that deceivers are capable of monitoring interactions and adapting their communicative behaviors when targets suspect the validity of their statements.

Further evidence of the influence of interrogative probes emerged from one of our recent investigations (Stiff, Corman, & Raghavendra, 1991). We employed interaction analysis procedures to examine the effects of an interviewer's probing questions on the nonverbal behavior of liars and truth-tellers. Participants in our study adopted the role of interviewer and interviewee; interviewees were asked to conceal or reveal their emotional reactions to a pair of film clips they had seen, and interviewers were instructed to ask probing questions to assess the interviewee's evaluation of the film clips.[1]

A coding scheme (adapted from Donohue, in press) was used to evaluate interviewer requests for information. The four categories in this coding scheme were developed to reflect levels of interviewer cognitive involvement with the interview (Table 6.2).

The first category of directives, *listening cues,* consists of verbal backchannels and simple restatements of an interviewee's prior response. This category reflects the lowest level of interviewer involvement, as these types of directives require little cognitive effort. The second category, *requesting directives,* asks the interviewee to provide specific information in response to a direct question. This category of directives reflects a greater level of cognitive involvement on the part of interviewers. *Evaluation directives* request an evaluative summary from interviewees, or provide an evaluative summary and ask interviewees to respond to it. This form of directive reflects greater cognitive involvement than a requesting directive, because it requires interviewers to recall and synthesize prior utterances of the interviewee. Finally, *framing directives* reflect the greatest level of cognitive involvement because they require interviewers to interpret prior utterances of the interviewee by referring to people, experiences, and situations that are outside the context of the interaction (Stiff et al., 1991, p. 9).

Using this coding scheme, we identified the amount of cognitive involvement exhibited by interviewers and related it to the nonverbal behaviors of interviewees. Our analyses produced an interesting pattern of results. First, we found that interviewers who displayed a high degree of cognitive involvement with the interview were more likely to judge the source as deceptive. We also found that interviewer information directives were positively related to interviewee response latencies ($\beta = .23$). That is, when interviewers used information directives that reflected a high degree of cognitive involvement with the interview,

TABLE 6.2

Definitions and Examples of Information Directives

1. Listening Cues: This type of information directive indicates that the interviewer is listening to the respondent and invites the respondent to continue talking. This category consists primarily of verbal backchannels including; uh huh, o.k., I see, yea, etc. Also included in this category are simple restatements of a prior utterance, or a portion of it.

EE: The film made me relaxed.
ER: O.K. ***
EE: Calm. It was soothing to watch.

ER: Did the first film and the second relate to each other in any way?
EE: Not really.
ER: O.K. ***
EE: They were pretty much different.

ER: How did the film make you feel?
EE: Relaxed.
ER: Relaxed? ***
EE: Yeah. It was soothing to watch.

ER: Were they boring or exciting?
EE: They were sick.
ER: They were sick? ***
EE: They were, well they weren't, I guess they were more exciting, and boring, and gross.

2. Requesting Directives: This category focuses on the act of requesting information. Statements in this category ask the respondent, more or less directly, to provide information. This category includes requests for information that do not ask for or provide an evaluation of prior utterances.

EE: It was enjoyable to watch, sorta.
ER: Can you describe the film in more detail? ***
EE: Not really, that's about it.

ER: Can you tell me more about it? ***
EE: Well, it was like I said . . .

3. Evaluation Directives: Directives in this category request information by (1) requesting an evaluative summary of a prior utterance or utterances, or (2) providing an evaluative summary and requesting a response to it. These directives indicate a higher level of involvement than simple requests because they require a specific evaluation of a prior utterance.

ER: So you're saying they were, that both film clips were basically the same format? ***
EE: Yeah, they, I thought it was strange what they were showing, but they were pretty much the same.

ER: So which film clip did you like the best? ***
EE: I liked them both about the same.

4. Framing Directives: This category contains statements that attempt to provide an *interpretation* for a prior utterance or utterances by referring to other experiences, situations, or people that are *outside the context of the interviewee's viewing of the film clips*. Framing directives indicate a higher level of cognitive involvement because they require the interviewer to think of and reference other experiences, situations, or people that may help provide an interpretation for the interviewee's utterances. Framing directives include analogies (references to similar people, situations and experiences, etc.) and hypothetical questions.

ER: Was it like when we went up north last summer? ***
EE: Yea, it was a lot like that.

ER: Do you think your mom would have liked it? ***
EE: [Laughs] Yea, right.

SOURCE: From "Truth Biases and Aroused Suspicion in Relational Deception," by J. B. Stiff, H. J. Kim & C. N. Ramesh, 1992, *Communication Research, 19*, pp. 326-345. Used by permission.
NOTE: Statements followed by three asterisks (***) are examples of directives in a particular category.

sources took more time to prepare their replies. In fact, the cognitive involvement of interviewer directives contributed almost as much to response latencies ($\beta = .23$) as the interviewee's actual message veracity ($\beta = .35$). Finally, we observed that sources with longer response latencies were likely to be judged as deceptive by their interview partners ($\beta = .23$). Together, our findings suggest that the more cognitive involvement targets displayed during the interview, the more likely they were to observe the longer latencies in their partner's responses, and subsequently, to judge their partner to be communicating deceptively. Though preliminary, these findings suggest that understanding the co-dependence of targets and sources is a central feature of deceptive transactions.

These findings have important practical implications as well. To the extent that information directives and replies are co-dependent, professional interviewers must recognize their influence on the responses of interviewees. Characteristics of an interviewer's questions may influence the verbal and nonverbal behaviors the interviewer relies on to make judgments about a source's veracity. A more complete understanding of these interactive effects may be necessary to increase our understanding of deceptive transactions.

DETECTING RELATIONAL DECEPTION

One of the most frequently cited criticisms of early research on deceptive communication stemmed from the fact that most studies investigated deception among strangers. Whether this was due to the convenience of the sample, ethical concerns about meddling with existing relationships, or even a disinterest in the relational consequences of deception, the fact that most studies involved deception among strangers meant that findings from these studies had limited generalizability for deceptive transactions involving close friends and relational partners. Indeed, one frequent response to the conclusion that humans are unable to detect deception accurately (see Chapter 5) is that most detection accuracy studies involved deception among strangers who should not be expected to detect each other's deception accurately.

In Chapter 4 we argued that while some deceptive behavior is consistent across people and situations, a sizeable portion of an individual's deceptive behavior may be idiosyncratic; that is, any individual's "deceptive code" is comprised of verbal and nonverbal cues that are common across people and some person-specific cues unique to the individual. Because friends and relational partners are privy to each other's idiosyncratic deceptive behavior, one might expect them to be more effective at detecting deception when it occurs.

Encouraged by the findings of a few early studies, several investigators have recently explored deception among close friends and intimates and examined the influence of relational factors on the detection process. In this section we will discuss strategies people use to detect deception perpetrated by a relational partner and compare the detection accuracy scores of strangers, friends, and intimates. We will then explore factors that hinder deception detection in close relationships.

Detection Strategies

In 1975, Miller and Steinberg articulated their developmental model of interpersonal communication. They argued that as relationships become more developed, partners rely less on cultural and sociological information and more on psychological information to make predictions about each other's behaviors. As relationships develop, people gain insights into the specific behavioral patterns of their partners. These insights are accumulated over time and represent a baseline by which subsequent interactions can be compared. This baseline information, which is typically unavailable to those outside the relationship, should aid deception detection. Recall that in Chapter 5 we argued that when these baselines were experimentally induced through repeated exposures to the same truthful behavior, strangers demonstrated improved detection accuracy.

Reliance on behavioral baselines was evidenced in a recent investigation employing survey research techniques (Miller, Mongeau, & Sleight, 1986). Miller et al. asked relationally involved couples to describe cues their partners exhibited that triggered their suspicions of deceit. Most respondents indicated that departures from their typical verbal or nonverbal behavior usually signaled a deception. Specifically, respondents indicated that *changes* in a partner's eye contact, hand and foot movements, and length of responses were likely to arouse suspicions of deceit. When asked to describe strategies for detecting deception by a relational partner and a stranger, respondents indicated that they considered both verbal and nonverbal behaviors to judge a partner, but concentrated primarily on the consistency of the verbal message when judging a stranger (1986, p.14).

Given the existence and use of these behavioral baselines, one might expect that, compared to strangers, relational partners would have a decided advantage in detecting deception. Nevertheless, investigations have found that people are no more accurate when making veracity judgments about relational partners than they are when judging strangers.

Detection Accuracy

The first investigation to compare the detection accuracy rates of strangers, friends, and intimates involved deception about both factual information and self-feelings (Bauchner, cited in Miller et al., 1981). Bauchner asked participants to present truthful and deceptive messages while a stranger, friend, and spouse watched through a one-way mirror. There were no differences in detection accuracy when observers judged factual messages. When judging self-feelings, however, friends were significantly more accurate than either strangers or spouses.

Comadena (1982) asked spouses in well-adjusted marriages to participate in interviews in which they provided truthful and deceptive descriptions of the factual content and their emotional reaction to a series of stimulus tapes. A friend was also present and served the role of observer. Following each interview the friend observer and spouse interviewer judged the veracity of the spouse who was interviewed. Comadena reported a very small difference ($\eta = .22$, $p < .07$) between the detection accuracy rates of friends and spouses. This small difference was attributed to female spouses who were significantly more accurate judges of deception than female friends.

Following the interviews, Comadena asked interviewers to watch a videotape of the interview and reevaluate their spouse's veracity. Analysis of these findings revealed that intimates were significantly more accurate when reevaluating emotional rather than factual content. Comadena speculated that "intimates saw and/or heard something the second time they viewed the messages that tipped them off to the deceptions" (1982, p. 468). Miller et al. (1986) offered an alternative explanation. They argued that passive observation permitted intimates to focus their attention entirely on the behaviors of the source, increasing the likelihood of accurate detection. A recent replication of the differences between active and passive observers provided additional support for this explanation (Buller, Strzyzewski, & Comstock, 1991).

Neither Bauchner nor Comadena found support for the claim that people are better able to detect deception from a relational partner than a stranger. Though relational partners have baseline information about one another, they apparently do not employ this information very effectively when making veracity judgments. One possible explanation for this state of affairs may stem from a lack of motivation to judge a relational partner as deceptive.

Truth Biases

McCornack and Parks (1986) introduced the construct *truth bias* and used it to explain the difficulty people have in detecting deception from a relational partner. The relational costs associated with accusing a partner of deception, combined with a disproportionate number of truthful interactions, lead people in intimate relationships to presume their partner is usually truthful. Findings from two studies were consistent with predictions about the influence of the truth bias (McCornack & Parks, 1986; Levine & McCornack, 1992). In these studies, a couple's level of relational development was positively related to the existence of a truth bias, which in turn was negatively related to detection accuracy.

We recently extended this analysis and reconceptualized the truth bias as a cognitive heuristic. Heuristics are simple decision rules people use to evaluate complex stimuli with little cognitive effort (Tversky & Kahneman, 1974). Applied in deceptive transactions, these rules of thumb are often used in lieu of careful evaluation of a source's verbal and nonverbal behavior. As relationships grow, the simple decision rule: "My partner has been truthful in the past, therefore he or she is being truthful now," becomes available and guides the evaluation of behavior (Stiff, Kim, & Ramesh, 1992, p. 328). In well-developed relationships, the truth bias heuristic becomes chronically accessible due to its constant use.

Our investigation of friendship and dating dyads found that relational development was positively associated with the truth bias heuristic. In addition, people who reported a strong truth bias exhibited significantly less cognitive involvement in an interview designed to detect deception perpetrated by a relational partner. Replicating the pattern of results in prior research, the truth bias heuristic was positively related to judgments of truthfulness and negatively related to detection accuracy. Finally, we also examined the influence of aroused suspicion on the truth bias heuristic. Consistent with our hypothesis, suspicion aroused by a third party offset the truth bias heuristic and increased judgments of deceit (Figure 6.2).

Findings from these studies provide a clear and compelling explanation for the inability of people to detect deception accurately from a relational partner. Armed with sufficient baseline information, relational partners passively rely on the truth bias as a means for making veracity judgments. However, suspicion aroused by a third party may be sufficient to reduce reliance on this heuristic and result in more effortful scrutiny of a partner's statements.

SUMMARY AND CONCLUSIONS

Though a number of situational factors may affect detection accuracy, four features have received the most attention from scholars of deceptive communication. Research on the detection of factual and emotional deception is the most sparse. Though far from conclusive, research involving strangers suggests that factual deception may be more easily detected than deception about self-feelings. Comadena found different effects for people in intimate relationships: for men, deceptive content had no effect on detection accuracy. Women in intimate relationships, however, were more likely to detect deception about self-feelings than factual deception.

Research on the differences between planned and spontaneous deception is equally mixed. Planning seems to reduce the cognitive effort required to produce a deceptive message, but it appears to have little effect on the arousal during message production. With regard to deception detection, it may be that the social interaction skills reflected in the

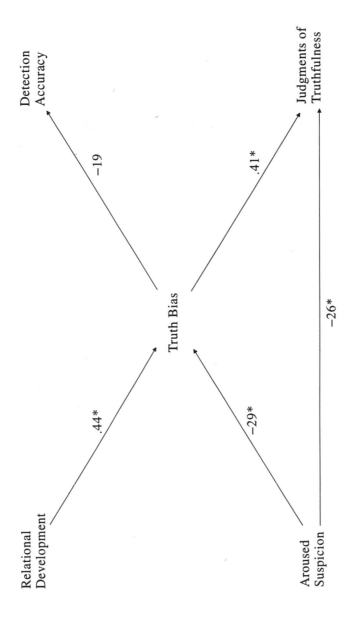

Figure 6.2. A Model of Depicting the Effects of Relational Development, Truth Bias, and Aroused Suspicion on Detection Accuracy and Judgments of Truthfulness
SOURCE: From "Truth Biases and Aroused Suspicion in Relational Deception," by J. B. Stiff, H. J. Kim, & C. N. Ramesh, 1992, *Communication Research, 19,* pp. 326-345. Used by permission.
NOTE: *p <.05

self-monitoring construct may moderate the relationship between rehearsal and deception effectiveness. High self-monitors may benefit from the time to plan and rehearse their deceptive messages. Conversely, low self-monitors may not benefit, and may even be less successful deceivers when given time to plan and rehearse their deceptions.

Interrogative probes have an important influence on the deception process. Two studies revealed the co-dependence of a target's questions and a source's responses in deceptive interactions. Interaction analysis procedures revealed that the use of highly involving probes can influence a deceiver's nonverbal behaviors and influence subsequent judgments of deception. In this regard, the questions asked by targets of deceptive messages may indirectly influence the veracity judgments they make. Though preliminary, these findings suggest that both deceivers and their targets may contribute significantly to the production of a deceiver's verbal and nonverbal behavior. Further application of interaction analysis procedures promises to expand our understanding of the role targets of deception play in the detection process.

Finally, investigations involving friends and intimates help explain why people have difficulty detecting deception perpetrated by relational partners. Though relational familiarity should provide partners with idiosyncratic information about one another, they are unwilling to use this information and rely instead on a truth bias heuristic for evaluating a partner's messages. Cognitive biases like the truth bias may serve to reduce the detection accuracy in many deceptive settings.

Further investigation of these and other situational factors is necessary if we are to understand the process of deception and deception detection more fully. Given that the majority of our daily interactions rest on the presumption of honesty, understanding of situational features that affect this presumption may be necessary to improve our ability to detect deception when it occurs.

NOTE

1. This study investigated the influence of an interviewer's questions on both the verbal and nonverbal behavior of respondents. For now, we will consider only the effects of interviewer directives on the *nonverbal* behavior of interviewees. In Chapter 7 we will examine *verbal* characteristics of the directive-reply sequences in this study.

7
Challenges for Future Research

In the preceding four chapters we reviewed some important findings from prior investigations of deceptive communication. Examination of this literature permitted us to confidently offer conclusions about some aspects of deceptive transactions, but left us uncertain about others. Our review included several cautionary notes about the utility of some research findings and the generalizability of others. In addition, we remain concerned about the paucity of theories that have been employed to develop an understanding of this important aspect of human interaction. Thus, in this final chapter, we revisit many of these issues and discuss some of the theoretical, methodological, and ethical issues that await future investigations of deceptive communication. To begin, we identify three specific challenges for future investigations and offer some methodological suggestions for meeting these challenges. Following this, we discuss several theoretical perspectives that promise to provide a more complete understanding of deceptive communication. Finally, we conclude the chapter with a consideration of several ethical dilemmas that underscore the difficulty of conducting effective and responsible investigations of this communicative process.

CHALLENGE I: IMPROVING THE GENERALIZABILITY OF DECEPTION RESEARCH

In Chapter 3 we discussed the merits of several categories of research procedures. Recall that we identified several essential features of naturally occurring deceptive transactions and criticized several procedures for failing to replicate these essential features in laboratory settings.

Perhaps the most important limitation of prior investigations stems from the deficient motivation of deceivers to communicate effectively and the deficient motivation of targets to detect deception when it occurs. Thus, our first challenge is to adopt research procedures that more closely approximate deception in naturally occurring transactions.

As we mentioned in Chapter 3, research participants who are asked to produce deceptive messages anticipate no retribution for failing to deceive effectively. As a result, there is no reason to expect that the levels of arousal and cognitive effort exhibited by these research participants match the levels of arousal and cognitive effort experienced by deceivers in most naturally occurring deceptive transactions. One solution to this problem is to move beyond these traditional procedures and employ research procedures in which participants are neither asked nor expected to communicate deceptively. The Exline procedure effectively achieves this goal. Recall from Chapter 2 that with this procedure, participants are faced with a decision about whether to cheat or honestly complete an experimental task. Participants who cheat face the decision to respond truthfully or deceptively to subsequent questions about their successful completion of the difficult experimental task. This procedure has been used successfully in two prior studies (deTurck & Miller, 1985; Stiff & Miller, 1986), and provides researchers with the benefits of experimental control while sacrificing little motivation on the part of deceivers.

In addition to refining experimental procedures, investigators must explore possibilities for studying deception as it naturally occurs. Investigative interviews are one avenue for field studies of deceptive communication. Law enforcement agencies frequently record investigative interviews of suspects, witnesses, and victims. In fact, many agencies record pre-polygraph and polygraph examinations. Such information provides fertile opportunities for researchers attempting to establish a link between deceptive behavior and physiological arousal. Employment interviews are another source of data for deception researchers. Employers routinely examine the work and personal histories of job applicants, and these interviews are often accompanied by a polygraph exam.

An important practical difficulty faces researchers who examine messages generated during investigative interviews; researchers must be cautious to categorize the veracity of interview participants accurately. Although researchers using the Exline procedure can be relatively certain of an interviewee's veracity, establishing the veracity of interviewees in naturally occurring interviews is a difficult task. Often subsequent casework can provide enough information to label an interviewee's behavior as mostly truthful, mostly deceptive, or indeterminant, but this casework is difficult to obtain and time consuming to review. Neverthe-less, accurate classification of an interviewee's veracity is critical because it is a criterion by which communicative behavior is evaluated.

Presently, we are investigating the communicative patterns of chil-dren who participate in child abuse forensic interviews. We were able to negotiate access with the director of a child abuse assessment center who desired a better understanding of the forensic interview process. After identifying the kinds of information we needed for the study, members of the child abuse assessment staff collected the interview data and removed the identifying features before releasing transcripts, de-mographic characteristics, and case histories to us for analysis. Thus we were able to obtain samples of investigative interviews and correspond-ing case information without compromising the privacy rights of chil-dren participating in these interviews.

Data collected in natural settings are difficult to obtain, but they offer the prospects of a richer understanding of the deception process. Coop-eration between researchers and agency staff is essential to the success of these projects and the privacy of interview participants. Of course, investigative interviews are only one example of naturally occurring transactions in which deception sometimes occurs. Creative thinking about other situations and opportunities for observing them will extend our understanding of this process.

CHALLENGE II: STUDYING DECEPTION AS A COMMUNICATIVE PROCESS

Researchers must also accept the challenge to move their investiga-tions beyond the static, linear conceptions of communication that dominated prior deception research, and conceptualize deceptive com-munication as an interactive process. For example, two earlier studies explored the influence of target probes on deceiver behavior (Buller, Strzyzewski, & Comstock, 1991; Stiff & Miller, 1986). Although they represented a move toward a more interactive paradigm, neither study employed methods of interaction analysis. Instead, both studies created categories of target probes and employed analysis of variance tech-niques to assess their influence on deceiver behavior. Thus these studies were a step in the right direction, but fell short of uncovering the interactive nature of deceptive interactions.

In a recent study we adopted a more interactive methodology to examine the influence of interviewer probes on deceiver behavior (Stiff et al., 1991). We found that a target's level of cognitive involvement in the interaction (as indicated by the complexity of interrogative probes) influenced the responsiveness and response latency of truthful and deceptive sources. To our knowledge, this was the first investigation that examined the influence of a target's verbal behavior on the verbal and nonverbal responses of deceptive message sources. Although this investigation emphasized the mutual influences of source and target on truthful and deceptive behavior, it failed to consider the processural nature of deceptive transactions.

To address this concern, our most recent investigation employed time series analysis to examine the patterns of nonverbal behavior associated with critical and noncritical interview probes (Stiff, Corman et al., 1992). Using a modified version of the Exline procedure, we provided students with an opportunity to cheat while grading a class quiz. As expected, more than 50% of the students were academically dishonest and inflated their actual score. Several weeks later we interviewed these students about a variety of academic issues, focusing on academic dishonesty.

Time series analysis permitted us to separate individual patterns of nonverbal behavior in each interview from patterned behavior that was generalizable across a class of people. For example, our analysis of truthful and deceptive sources revealed that a considerable amount of variation in response latency was due to idiosyncratic patterns of nonverbal behavior. After modeling these individual patterns of behavior and controlling their effects, we unveiled a more sophisticated pattern of nonverbal behavior than had been previously realized in deception research. We found that nonverbal responses to critical probing questions were acute, but decayed quickly. For example, our analysis of response latencies revealed that a series of decaying spikes was associated with the pattern of an interviewer's critical questions.

Though preliminary, these findings suggest that traditional pre-post intervention models may inadequately represent changes in nonverbal behavior during deceptive transactions. In other words, limitations imposed by antiquated analytical techniques may help explain the inconsistent findings of researchers who have attempted to catalog nonverbal correlates of deception. For example, traditional pre-post ANOVA models produced null effects in our most recent study but an interesting combination of idiosyncratic and generalizable behavior emerged when time series models were employed to analyze the same deceptive transactions (Stiff, Corman et al., 1992). As a result, we strongly recommend a move beyond traditional analysis of variance procedures toward adoption of time-based analytical models like time series analysis.

CHALLENGE III: INVESTIGATING
VERBAL DECEPTIVE BEHAVIOR

Until recently, scholars of deceptive communication have exhibited a preoccupation with nonverbal behavior. While many investigations sought to isolate nonverbal correlates of deceptive behavior, only a handful of studies have examined characteristics of verbal statements that are associated with deceptive messages and judgments of deception. Combined with our conclusion in Chapter 6 that verbal statements may be more reliable indicators of deceit than nonverbal behavior, the lack of attention given verbal cues leads us to recommend more frequent investigation of both verbal *and* nonverbal characteristics of truthful and deceptive messages.

Recently, two research programs evolved in different scholarly fields that focus attention on verbal characteristics of deceptive communication. Although we recommend development of research programs that integrate the study of verbal and nonverbal behavior, these recent developments reflect a renewed awareness of the importance of verbal components of deceptive messages.

Conversational Norms and Deceptive Communication

The first comprehensive effort to examine verbal characteristics of deception was met with limited success (Bavelas et al., 1990). Though we voiced reservations about the wisdom of adopting a linguistic definition of deception (see Chapter 2), the Bavelas et al. approach reflected movement away from traditional models for investigating deceptive communication.

Since then, a promising avenue of research was paved by McCornack (1992), who applied Grice's (1989) discussion of conversational maxims to the study of deceptive communication. Grice (1989) argued that participants in communicative transactions are expected to adhere to a Cooperative Principle, defined specifically by four conversational maxims. The *quantity* maxim suggests that participants should provide an appropriate amount of information to meet the situational requirement of the interaction. Violations of this maxim occur when participants either provide excessive information, or fail to fulfill the informational requirements of the interaction. The *quality* maxim suggests that interactants are expected to refrain from providing information they know to be false or inaccurate. The *relevance* maxim suggests that interactants are expected to contribute information that is relevant to the topic or issue addressed in the preceding utterances. Finally, the *manner* maxim reflects the expectation that interactants will provide information in a concise, orderly fashion and attempt to avoid ambiguity and confusion.

McCornack (1992) noted that deceptive communication, by its very nature, is a noncooperative form of interaction. As such, the production of deceptive messages results in subtle violations of the conversational rules that govern cooperative interaction. This reasoning gave rise to the fundamental principle of McCornack's analysis: "Messages that are commonly thought of as deceptive derive from covert violations of the conversational maxims" (1992, p. 5).

As a preliminary test of his analysis, McCornack, Levine, Solowcsuk, Torres, and Campbell (1992) asked participants to read messages that manipulated the extent to which each of Grice's conversational maxims was violated. Messages that violated the quantity, quality, relevance, and clarity (manner) maxims were perceived to be more deceptive than a fully disclosive message that did not violate these maxims. This preliminary evidence supports McCornack's reasoning that messages violating Grice's (1989) cooperative principle are likely to create perceptions of deception.

Using data from *actual* truthful and deceptive interactions, we recently tested McCornack's proposition that violations of conversational maxims are likely to engender perceptions of deception (Stiff et al., 1991). Recall from Chapter 6 that participants in this study adopted the role of interviewer and interviewee; interviewees were asked to conceal or reveal their emotional reactions to a pair of film clips, and interviewers were instructed to ask probing questions to assess the interviewee's evaluation of the film clips. We used the coding scheme described in Chapter 6 to code the information directives of interviewers (see Table 6.2).

This study also required the development of a coding scheme to evaluate interviewee replies to interrogative probes. We applied McCornack's (1992) reasoning and developed a coding scheme based on the expectation that violations of Grice's (1989) relevance and quantity maxims

TABLE 7.1

Definitions and Examples of Interviewee Replies

1. Nonresponsive Replies: These replies are not responsive to the interviewer's request for information. They include implicit or explicit refusals to answer questions, challenges to the interviewer's right to ask a question, and laughs (and other audibles) that cannot be coded in a higher category.

ER: Um, what's the major thought that you thought while you were in there?
EE: Are these questions they gave you to ask? ***

ER: Why can't you tell me about it?
EE: I don't know! ***

ER: What were you thinking during the film clip?
EE: I'm hungry and late for dinner. Do you have much more? ***

ER: What were you feeling while you watched the film?
EE: I don't think you're supposed to ask me that. ***

ER: What did you like most about it?
EE: [Interviewee laughs] ***

2. Irrelevant Replies: Responses in this category include statements that seem related to the general issue being discussed, but are not relevant to the interviewer's specific information directive. Such responses can take the form of an explicit topic shift, but are often more subtle deviations from the specific issue being discussed. The key question is: "Is the information provided relevant to the *prior* information directive?"

ER: Was the first one interesting to watch?
EE: They both contained scenes of children playing in the park. ***

ER: What were they about, what's the first one about?
EE: Cancer and doing autopsies on cancer people.
ER: Was it disgusting, was it sickening?
EE: And then they showed um, kids that were in a, they had been bombed by these Lebanon. ***

3. Relevant and Responsive Replies: This category includes utterances that meet the obligation of providing relevant information requested by the prior utterance. The information contained in the response may be minimal, or it may be fairly extensive.

ER: How did you feel after watching the film?
EE: Happy. ***

ER: Happy, um, was it happy because, the movie, the, the clip was enjoyable to watch or not?
EE: It was enjoyable to watch, sorta. ***

ER: Was the first one better than the second?
EE: Yea, I thought it was a little better. ***

4. Elaborative Replies: Responses in this category meet the obligation of providing information that is directly relevant to the prior directive and additional information that goes beyond the topic of the prior directive. In most cases, responses in this category take the form of complex or compound sentences. That is, one clause is relevant to the information directive and the other provides additional information that is not directly relevant.

ER: Was there music with the second film clip?
EE: Yea, they played classical music that was easy to listen to. ***

ER: Did they show animals in both film clips?
EE: They showed animals in the wild and scenes of people going to work in the morning. ***

ER: Can you tell me what the first film clip was about?
EE: They showed dead babies and I didn't enjoy watching it much. ***

SOURCE: From "Exploring the Process of Deception Detection," paper presented by J. B. Stiff, S. R. Corman, and S. Raghavendra at the annual meeting of the International Communication Association, Chicago, May, 1991. Used by permission.
NOTE: Statements followed by three asterisks (***) are examples of replies in the particular category.

would produce judgments of deception. Thus, we created four categories of replies (Table 7.1). *Nonresponsive replies* violated Grice's (1989) quantity and relevance maxims, as they failed to provide the relevant information expected from the interviewer's prior utterance. *Irrelevant replies* provided information that was *globally* relevant to the issue being discussed, but not *locally* relevant to the preceding utterance. As such, responses in this category violated the relevance maxim, but not the quantity maxim. *Relevant and responsive replies* provided a sufficient quantity of relevant information to fulfill the expectation created by the prior information directive. These replies violated neither the relevance nor quantity maxim. Finally, *elaborative replies* met the relevance requirement, but violated the quantity requirement by providing more information than was expected from the preceding information directive (Stiff et al., 1991, p. 7).

We found preliminary indications of a more complex pattern of conversational expectancies than is apparent in McCornack's analysis of Grice's cooperative principle. Specifically, the meanings people assign to violations of Grice's conversational maxims may be dependent on the expectations created by the preceding information directive. For example, we found that nonresponsive replies to requesting directives were more likely to engender perceptions of deception than nonresponsive replies to other types of information directives. In addition, we found that failure to violate one of these maxims may also engender perceptions of deception. Sources who used relevant and responsive replies most frequently in response to framing directives were more likely to be judged deceptive than sources who used these replies in response to all forms of information directives (Stiff et al., 1991, p. 21). Though preliminary, these findings provide further support for McCornack's (1992) argument that conversational expectations drive the meanings people assign to verbal responses of liars and truthtellers.

Statement Validity Analysis

Recent efforts by communication scholars to better understand verbal aspects of deceptive messages coincide with efforts by child psychologists and child abuse case workers who are working to develop procedures for assessing the validity of children's testimony in sexual abuse cases. The credibility of witness testimony plays a critical role in the legal resolution of child sexual abuse cases. Often the testimony of children in these cases is received with a large dose of skepticism. In an attempt to evaluate the veracity of children's accusations of child abuse accurately, researchers in Germany proposed Criteria Based Content Analysis (CBCA), an analytical technique that examines verbal accounts of children (Undeutsch, 1989; Wegener, 1989). Based on more than 30 years of case experience, CBCA proposed that five categories of verbal content may reliably distinguish truthful and deceptive accounts of child sexual abuse.

Several descriptions of these criteria have appeared in the literature (Raskin & Esplin, 1991; Steller & Koehnken, 1989), and a brief description of them is provided below. The first category of criteria assesses general characteristics of the child's statement; emphasizing its coherence, logical structure, quantity and quality of details, and whether the statement is somewhat disorganized and unconstrained. The second category examines the specific content of the child's descriptions; that is, description of specific conversations, reproduction of specific statements, evidence of spatial or temporal contextualization of events, statements of unexpected complications during the incident. The third category looks for peculiar features of the child's description. For example, the recall of peripheral details that are relevant to the situation but not to the alleged event, inclusion of unusual details or descriptions of people, descriptions of feelings or emotions experienced during the alleged event, and attributions about the alleged perpetrator's feelings or motives. The fourth category of criteria assesses the child's motivation for making the accusation. Spontaneous corrections, self-doubt about the believability of the statement, self-blame, and willingness to forgive (or failure to blame) the perpetrator may indicate the child's concern for the truth and disinterest in prompting punitive action against the alleged perpetrator. The final category looks for specific details that are characteristic of the type of offense and perpetrator being alleged.

Investigations have recently begun to examine the validity of CBCA by using it to distinguish between truthful and fabricated statements of children. Investigations using story-telling procedures (Steller, Wellershaus, & Wolfe, 1988) and child abuse forensic interviews (Boychuk, 1991; Raskin & Esplin, 1991) found that truthful statements, or statements with a high probability of being truthful, contained significantly more of the characteristic features described by the coding scheme than deceptive statements, or statements that had a high probability of being fabricated. For example, in the Boychuk study several of these criteria were present in 95% or more of the forensic interviews for which corresponding casework indicated a high probability that the child was communicating truthfully. Conversely, many of these same criteria were present in less than 30% of cases in which there was a high probability that the child's accusation was fabricated. These findings suggest that scrutiny of verbal content may provide insights into the deception detection process. If CBCA proves to be valid, it will greatly assist child abuse case workers who struggle with the difficult task of assessing the validity of children's accusations. In combination, investigations of conversational norms and statement validity analysis promise to provide a more complete understanding of the role of verbal statements in truthful and deceptive transactions. Though preliminary, these efforts redirect attention toward the important role of verbal content in deception and deception detection.

THEORETICAL PERSPECTIVES FOR
FUTURE DECEPTION RESEARCH

To confront these challenges successfully, deception scholars must be willing to adapt relevant theoretical perspectives from other studies of human behavior. While the development of a "theory of deceptive communication" may be unnecessary, scholars may gain considerable benefit from adapting recent theoretical advances in related areas of inquiry. As evidence of our position, we describe three theoretical perspectives that seem able to further our understanding of deceptive transactions.

First, theories of arousal and cognition may provide a better understanding of the role of nonverbal behavior in these transactions. Arousal has traditionally played a dominant role in the explanation of nonverbal behaviors associated with deception (see, deTurck & Miller, 1985; Zuckerman et al., 1981; Zuckerman & Driver, 1985). However, the specific theoretical relationship between various types of physiological arousal and particular nonverbal behaviors has yet to be identified. In addition, the empirical relationship between arousal and particular nonverbal behaviors has recently been challenged (Sparks & Greene, 1992). Cognitive theories have also been employed to explain the association between certain vocal cues and deceptive communication (Cody et al., 1984; Greene et al., 1985); however, more conceptual work remains to be done in this area as well. Perhaps the greatest challenge that faces scholars of deception is the eventual integration of arousal and cognitive explanations of nonverbal cues that emerge in deceptive transactions.

A second genre of theories that offers promise for deception scholars has attempted to explain the attributions people make about adherence to and violation of conversational norms. Conceptual work by Grice (1989) and Bavelas et al. (1990) has recently been applied to examine the sociolinguistic features of truthful and deceptive messages. Though preliminary, several investigations (Bavelas et al., 1990; McCornack et al., 1992; Stiff et al., 1991) found that people have expectations about normative interaction, and that these expectations affect veracity judgments made by conversational participants. While many questions remain about the influence of specific violations of conversational norms and the meanings interactants derive from them, these theoretical developments provide another avenue for further understanding the verbal characteristics of deceptive messages.

In addition to applying these theories for understanding micro-level verbal and nonverbal behavior, research on social cognition can easily be applied to the study of deception. Research ranging from cognitive construct categories (Bargh & Pratto, 1986) to the use of cognitive heuristics (Chaiken, 1987) can be effectively used to understand how people make general assessments about another person's honesty. Investigations of truth biases in developed relationships (Stiff, Kim, & Ramesh, 1992) provide one example of how these cognitive processes can help explain the deception detection process.

These three abbreviated descriptions provide examples of the potential that theories of arousal, cognition, and sociolinguistics offer for scholars of deceptive communication. No doubt, these theoretical perspectives, and others like them, are essential to meeting our fundamental challenge to develop theoretically based investigations of deceptive transactions.

ETHICAL CONCERNS ABOUT FUTURE DECEPTION RESEARCH

As scholars of deceptive communication, we routinely encounter questions about the ethics of studying deceptive communication. These questions frequently cause us to revisit important issues surrounding the ethical conduct of our research. Given the importance of these issues for current and future programs of deception research, we chose to conclude the book with a discussion of several important ethical dilemmas that confront deception scholars. Our discussion will not attempt to address the larger philosophical issues surrounding the ethics of lying and deceit. Such a discussion is beyond our expertise and the scope of this book, though we encourage interested readers to review Sissela Bok's (1979) thorough and insightful discussion of these issues. Instead, the present discussion will focus on the ethical concerns scholars face while investigating deceptive communication.

Because investigations of deceptive communication involve the use of research participants, they are subject to federal and local guidelines governing research involving human subjects. In addition to the general concerns explicitly stated in these guidelines, the research challenges we just identified call to mind several specific concerns about the ethical conduct of deception research. Indeed, research procedures that most closely approximate the essential characteristics of naturally occurring deceptive transactions, or that observe deception as it naturally occurs, provide additional ethical challenges for deception scholars.

Informed Consent. Informed consent is a standard requirement for research involving human subjects. Research procedures that are not part of a participant's everyday activities or that pose even minimal risk require informed consent from participants or their guardians. Informed consent procedures typically involve disclosure of the study's purpose, description of the activities involved in the research, specification of any compensation for participation, and a statement that the participant can freely withdraw from the study at any point in time.

It is often feasible to disclose the specific purpose of a study prior to participant participation. In many cases, however, full disclosure can undermine a study's effectiveness. Knowledge of a study's hypotheses, for example, may influence the nature of participant behavior. This is especially true of deception experiments that create an environment in which participants choose to communicate deceptively. In these cases, researchers and human subjects review boards must weigh the potential harmful effects of participation against the likely benefits the study will produce. Often it is permissible to deceive participants or to provide only "partial disclosure," as long as the general activities are described and the potential harmful effects are discussed. In either case, a complete debriefing of the research procedures is critical at the end of a study.

Two concerns about informed consent are specific to studies that employ investigative interviews as examples of truthful and deceptive behavior. First, investigators must be careful not to pressure interview participants to consent to including their interview in the study. Investigative interviews frequently occur in settings that are emotionally and legally charged. Under these circumstances, interview participants may be susceptible to even subtle pressures from eager researchers hoping to gain access to another interview. Second, participants in studies like this may not be available for debriefing. For example, participants in police investigative interviews who agree to have their interview included as part of a subsequent investigation of communicative behavior may not be accessible for a debriefing session following the interview. In other instances, such interaction may be socially or legally inappropriate. When it becomes extremely difficult to provide a complete debriefing statement to these interview participants, every effort must be made to provide a complete and accurate description of the study's purpose before acquiring informed consent.

Investigator Use of Deception. The challenge to improve the generalizability of our investigations has led to the development of several experimental procedures that involve the use of investigator deception. For example, in Chapter 3 we argued that the Exline procedure effectively replicated several essential characteristics of naturally occurring deceptive transactions. This procedure, however, involves the use of investigator deception. In order to create a situation in which deception is not sanctioned by the experimenter, and in which the experimenter can verify the veracity of a message, researchers using the Exline procedure are themselves deceptive when they describe the experimental procedures. Recall that this procedure involves the use of an experimental confederate, who is introduced as another student, and suggests that the naive participant cheat on the experimental task. The effectiveness of this procedure depends on the quality of the deception perpetrated by the researchers and the experimental confederate.

Though the level of experimenter deception is relatively high in this procedure, institutional review boards will often approve this procedure because it is necessary to increase the validity of research findings (i.e., unsanctioned deception), and places the participants at minimal psychological risk. Recently, we devised a somewhat less deceptive experimental procedure (Stiff, Corman et al., 1992, described earlier in this chapter) that permitted us to observe unsanctioned deceptive behavior of college students who were motivated to deceive effectively. Though this procedure is relatively complicated, it offers an alternative to researchers who are concerned about the use of deception in social science research. Though a variety of research procedures like these are presently available, and more are certain to be developed, it has been our experience that the more closely experimental procedures approximate deception in naturally occurring deceptive transactions, the more likely they are to involve the use of investigator deception. Though it may be necessary, the decision to adopt a procedure involving deception perpetrated by researchers should not be taken lightly, as the implications of such a decision can be far reaching (Bok, 1979).

Potential Risk. Two challenges raised earlier in this chapter—improving the generalizability of research findings and better study of deception as a communicative process—raise concerns about potential risk of our investigations for study participants. Specifically, studies investigating unsanctioned deception in highly motivating circumstances run the risk of harm to research participants. The potential for detrimental effects can take a variety of forms. Researchers must be concerned with the confidentiality of study findings, and in some cases the anonymity of research participants. For example, the academic dishonesty procedure we described earlier (Stiff, Corman et al., 1992) has the potential of placing students who cheated while grading their quiz at risk. If the course instructor had knowledge of the students who cheated while grading their quiz, then the possibility would have existed for retribution against the cheaters. To ensure that participants placed themselves at no risk, the instructor in our study was completely unaware of how many or which students were academically dishonest.

The concern of confidentiality and anonymity becomes even greater in field research. Investigation of child abuse accusations in forensic interviews exemplifies this concern. It is imperative that names and other identifying features be removed from these interviews before researchers examine them. In addition to protecting the privacy of children, care must be taken to protect the identity of people described in these accusations. In short, the investigators must ensure the privacy of all parties involved in the cases.

In addition to protecting the privacy of interactants, research in field settings must strive to minimize the trauma or psychological risks associated with participation in the research project. If a person's participation is limited to providing access to an interview that is normally occurring, then the likely psychological or emotional consequences of participating may be minimal. However, when participation includes activities that go beyond the typical investigative interview, researchers must be cautious not to place participants at increased risk of emotional or psychological problems stemming from their participation.

Another potential source of risk confronts participants in studies of relational deception. Although this issue has not been widely discussed in the literature, procedures that instigate deception between relational partners may produce unanticipated relational outcomes. Partners in a highly intimate relationship may grow to distrust one another, or become more skeptical of each other's veracity, after learning in an experiment they have been easily deceived. Though one might argue that increased suspicion may be healthy for certain relationships, researchers should be concerned about procedures that may produce these unintended effects. This concern is perhaps one reason why researchers have largely avoided extensive investigations of relational deception.

Application of Findings. A final ethical question facing investigators of deceptive communication is what should we do with the findings of our research? Investigations have isolated verbal and nonverbal correlates of deception, uncovered interview techniques for detecting deception, and found responses that may be effective for avoiding detection. Recently, scholars have shown that these findings can be effectively taught to targets of deception (deTurck, Harszlak, Bodhorn, & Texter, 1990; deTurck & Miller, 1990; Zuckerman et al., 1984). Given that we can teach people to deceive effectively and enable them to detect deception more accurately, we must ponder the question, "When, if ever, should findings from deception investigations be applied to train people to deceive and detect deception in naturally occurring transactions?" How accurate must our findings be before we employ them to inform juries and judges about the veracity of witnesses' testimony? More specifically, when should our understanding of children's accounts of sexual abuse become part of the legal proceedings to convict a person of child abuse?

Though the present discussion is unlikely to resolve this ethical dilemma adequately, two issues warrant consideration. First, the flip side of this question bears mentioning. "When, if ever, should we train people to tell the truth effectively and to detect truthfulness when it occurs?" Because most deception studies use truthful behavior as a criterion, findings from these studies are equally informative about truthful communication. As such, these results can also be applied to improve the believability and recognition of truthful messages. Thus, while some people may oppose the application of findings to enhance the process of deceptive communication, few would quarrel with their application to enhance truthful communication. Certainly, truthful communicators—for example, victims testifying in a courtroom—stand to benefit as much from our understanding of "deceptive communication" as their less honest counterparts.

A second issue concerns the ethics of deception itself. Although we stated earlier in this chapter that we would not attempt to resolve the ethical questions surrounding deceptive communication, resolution of these ethical issues is necessary before one can fully address the merits of training people to deceive and detect deception. If deceptive communication is deemed unacceptable in any situation, then it follows that training people to deceive more effectively is equally unacceptable. However, if deception is justified in some situations, then the use of training procedures to enhance a deceiver's effectiveness in those situations may be equally justified.

References

Allport, G. W., & Postman, L. J. (1945). The basic psychology of rumor. *Transactions of the New York Academy of Sciences, Series II, 8,* 61-81.

Bargh, J. A., & Pratto, F. (1986). Individual construct accessibility and perceptual selection. *Journal of Experimental Social Psychology, 22,* 293-311.

Bauchner, J. E., Brandt, D. R., & Miller, G. R. (1977). The truth/deception attribution: Effects of varying levels of information availability. In B. R. Ruben (Ed.), *Communication yearbook 1* (pp. 229-243). New Brunswick, NJ: Transaction Books.

Bauchner, J. E., Kaplan, E. P., & Miller, G. R. (1980). Detecting deception: The relationship of available information to judgmental accuracy in initial encounters. *Human Communication Research, 6,* 251-264.

Bavelas, J. B., Black, A., Chovil, N., & Mullett, J. (1990). *Equivocal communication.* Newbury Park, CA: Sage.

Berger, C. R. (1988). Planning, action, and social action generation. In L. Donohew, H. Sypher, & E. T. Higgins (Eds.), *Communication, social cognition, and affect.* Hillsdale, NJ: Lawrence Erlbaum.

Berlo, D. K., Lemert, J. B., & Mertz, R. J. (1969-1970). Dimensions for evaluating the acceptability of message sources. *Public Opinion Quarterly, 33,* 563-576.

Bok, S. (1979). *Lying: Moral choice in public and private life.* New York: Vintage.

Boychuk, T. D. (1991). *Criteria-based content analysis of children's statements about sexual abuse: A field-based validation study.* Unpublished doctoral dissertation, Arizona State University.

Brandt, D. R., Miller, G. R., & Hocking, J. E. (1980a). Effects of self-monitoring and familiarity on deception detection. *Communication Quarterly, 28,* 3-10.

Brandt, D. R., Miller, G. R., & Hocking, J. E. (1980b). The truth deception attribution: Effects of familiarity on the ability of observers to detect deception. *Human Communication Research, 6,* 99-110.

Brandt, D. R., Miller, G. R., & Hocking, J. E. (1982). Familiarity and lie detection: A replication and extension. *Western Journal of Speech Communication, 46,* 276-290.

Buller, D. B., Comstock, J., Aune, R. K., & Strzyzewski, K. D. (1989). The effect of probing on deceivers and truthtellers. *Journal of Nonverbal Behavior, 13,* 155-170.

Buller, D. B., Strzyzewski, K. D., & Comstock, J. (1991). Interpersonal deception I: Deceivers' reactions to receivers' suspicions and probing. *Communication Monographs, 58,* 1-24.

Buller, D. B., Strzyzewski, K. D., & Hundaker, F. G. (1991). Interpersonal deception II: The inferiority of conversational participants as deception detectors. *Communication Monographs, 58,* 25-40.

Chaiken, S. (1987). The heuristic model of persuasion. In M. P. Zanna, J. M. Olson, & C. P. Herman (Eds.), *Social influence: The Ontario symposium* (Vol. 5, pp. 3-39). Hillsdale, NJ: Lawrence Erlbaum.

Chaiken, S., & Eagly, A. H. (1983). Communication modality as a determinant of persuasion: The role of communicator salience. *Journal of Personality and Social Psychology, 45,* 241-256.

Chappell, M. N. (1929). Blood pressure changes in deception. *Archives in Psychology, 17,* 5-39.

Cody, M. J., Marston, P. J., & Foster, M. (1984). Deception: Paralinguistic and verbal leakage. In R. N. Bostrom (Ed.), *Communication yearbook 8* (pp. 464-490). Beverly Hills, CA: Sage.

Cody, M. J., & O'Hair, H. D. (1983). Nonverbal communication and deception: Differences in deception cues due to gender and communicator dominance. *Communication Monographs, 50,* 175-192.

Collins, R. L., Taylor, S. E., Wood, S. C., & Thompson, S. C. (1988). The vividness effect: Elusive or illusory? *Journal of Experimental Social Psychology, 24,* 1-18.

Comadena, M. E. (1982). Accuracy in detecting deception: Intimate and friendship relationships. In M. Burgoon (Ed.), *Communication yearbook 6* (pp. 446-472). Beverly Hills, CA: Sage.

Crowne, D., & Marlow, D. (1964). *The approval motive: Studies in evaluative dependence.* New York: John Wiley.

DePaulo, B. M., Davis, T., & Lanier, K. (1980, April). *Planning lies: The effects of spontaneity and arousal on success at deception.* Paper presented at the annual meeting of the Eastern Psychological Association, Hartford, CT.

DePaulo, B. M., Lanier, K., & Davis, T. (1983). Detecting deceit of the motivated liar. *Journal of Personality and Social Psychology, 45,* 1096-1103.

DePaulo, B. M., Stone, J. I., & Lassiter, G. D. (1985). Telling ingratiating lies: Effects of target sex and target attractiveness on verbal and nonverbal deceptive success. *Journal of Personality and Social Psychology, 48,* 1191-1203.

DePaulo, B. M., Zuckerman, M., & Rosenthal, R. (1980). Humans as lie detectors. *Journal of Communication, 30,* 129-139.

deTurck, M. A., Harszlak, J. J., Bodhorn, D. J., & Texter, L. A. (1990). The effects of training social perceivers to detect deception from behavioral cues. *Communication Quarterly, 38,* 189-199.

deTurck, M. A., & Miller, G. R. (1985). Deception and arousal: Isolating the behavioral correlates of deception. *Human Communication Research, 12,* 181-201.

deTurck, M. A., & Miller, G. R. (1990). Training observers to detect deception: Effects of self-monitoring and rehearsal. *Human Communication Research, 16,* 603-620.

DeVito, J. A., & Hecht, M. L. (1990). *The nonverbal communication reader.* Prospect Heights, IL: Waveland.

Dillard, J. P. (1990). A goal-driven model of interpersonal influence. In J. P. Dillard (Ed.), *Seeking compliance: The production of interpersonal influence messages* (pp. 41-56). Scottsdale, AZ: Gorsuch Scarisbrick.

Donohue, W. A. (in press). *Communication, marital dispute, and divorce mediation.* Hillsdale, NJ: Lawrence Erlbaum.

Eck, M. (1970). *Lies and truth.* London: Collier-Macmillan.

Ekman, P. (1985). *Telling lies: Clues to deceit in the marketplace, politics, and marriage.* New York: Norton.

Ekman, P., & Friesen, W. V. (1969). Nonverbal leakage and clues to deception. *Psychiatry, 32,* 88-106.

Ekman, P., & Friesen, W. V. (1972). Hand movements and deception. *Journal of Communication, 22,* 353-374.

Ekman, P., & Friesen, W. V. (1974). Detecting deception from the body or face. *Journal of Personality and Social Psychology, 20,* 288-298.

Ekman, P., & O'Sullivan, M. (1991). Who can catch a liar? *American Psychologist, 46,* 913-920.

Elliott, G. C. (1979). Some effects of deception and level of self-monitoring on planning and reacting to a self-presentation. *Journal of Personality and Social Psychology, 37,* 1282-1292.

Exline, R. E., Thibaut, J., Hickey, C. B., & Gumpert, P. (1970). Visual interaction in relation to Machiavellianism and an unethical act. In R. Christie & F. L. Geis (Eds.), *Studies in Machiavellianism* (pp. 53-75). New York: Academic Press.

Feldman, R. S. (Ed.). (1982). *Development of nonverbal behavior in children.* New York: Springer.

Feldman, R. S., Devin-Sheehan, L., & Allen, V. L. (1978). Nonverbal cues as indicators of verbal dissembling. *American Educational Research Journal, 15,* 217-231.

Gouldner, A. W. (1960). The reciprocity norm: A preliminary statement. *American Sociological Review, 25,* 161-178.

Greene, J. O. (1984). A cognitive approach to human communication: An action assembly theory. *Communication Monographs, 51,* 289-306.

Greene, J. O., O'Hair, D., Cody, M. J., & Yen, C. (1985). Planning and control of behavior during deception. *Human Communication Research, 11,* 335-364.

Grice, H. P. (1989). *Studies in the way of words.* Cambridge, MA: Harvard University Press.

Gustafson, L. A., & Orne, M. T. (1963). Effects of heightened motivation on the detection of deception. *Journal of Personality and Social Psychology, 47,* 408-411.

Hocking, J. E., Bauchner, J., Kaminski, E. P., & Miller, G. R. (1979). Detecting deceptive communication from verbal, visual, and paralinguistic cues. *Human Communication Research, 6,* 33-46.

Insko, C. A., Turnbull, W., & Yandell, B. (1974). Facilitative and inhibiting effects of distraction on attitude change. *Sociometry, 37,* 508-528.

Jones, E. E. (1964). *Ingratiation.* New York: Appleton-Century-Crofts.

Jones, E. E., & Wortman, C. (1972). *Ingratiation: An attributional approach.* Morristown, NJ: General Learning Press.

Kahneman, D., Slovic, P., & Tversky, A. (1982). *Judgment under uncertainty: Heuristics and biases.* Cambridge: Cambridge University Press.

Kalbfleisch, P. J. (1985). *Accuracy in deception detection: A quantitative review.* Unpublished doctoral dissertation, Michigan State University, East Lansing.

Knapp, M. L., & Comadena, M. E. (1979). Telling it like it isn't: A review of theory and research on deceptive communications. *Human Communication Research, 5,* 270-285.

Knapp, M. L., Hart, R. P., & Dennis, H. S. (1974). An exploration of deception as a communication construct. *Human Communication Research, 1,* 15-29.

Krauss, R. M., Apple, W., Morency, N., Wenzel, C., & Winton, W. (1981). Verbal, vocal, and visible factors in judgments of another's affect. *Journal of Personality and Social Psychology, 40,* 312-320.

Kraut, R. (1978). Verbal and nonverbal cues in the perception of lying. *Journal of Personality and Social Psychology, 36,* 380-391.

Kraut, R. (1980). Humans as lie detectors. *Journal of Communication, 30,* 209-216.

Kraut, R., & Poe, D. (1980). Behavioral roots of person perception: The deception judgments of customs inspectors and laymen. *Journal of Personality and Social Psychology, 39,* 784-798.

Lennox, R. D., & Wolfe, R. N. (1984). Revision of the self-monitoring scale. *Journal of Personality and Social Psychology, 46,* 1349-1364.

Levine, T. R., & McCornack, S. A. (1992). Linking love and lies: A formal test of the McCornack & Parks model of deception detection. *Journal of Social and Personal Relationships, 9,* 143-154.

Littlepage, G. E., & Pineault, M. A. (1979). Detection of deceptive factual statements from the body and face. *Personality and Social Psychology Bulletin, 5,* 325-328.

Littlepage, G. E., & Pineault, M. A. (1982). *Detection of deception of planned and spontaneous communications.* Unpublished paper, Department of Psychology, Middle Tennessee State University, Murfreesboro.

Locke, E. A. (1986). Generalizing from laboratory to field: Ecological validity or abstraction of essential elements? In E. A. Locke (Ed.), *Generalizing from laboratory to field settings* (pp. 5-9). Lexington, MA: Lexington Books.

Ludwig, A. M. (1965). *The importance of lying.* Springfield, IL: Charles C Thomas.

Lykken, D. T. (1974). Psychology and the lie detector industry. *American Psychologist, 29,* 725-739.

Lykken, D. T. (1978). The psychopath and the lie detector. *Psychophysiology, 15,* 137-142.

Maier, N. R. F., & Janzen, J. C. (1967). Reliability of reasons used in making judgments of honesty and dishonesty. *Perceptual and Motor Skills, 25,* 141-151.

Maier, N. R. F., & Thurber, J. (1968). Accuracy of judgments of deception when an interview is watched, heard, and read. *Personnel Psychology, 21,* 23-30.

Matarazzo, J. D., Wiens, A. N., Jackson, R. H., & Manaugh, T. S. (1970). Interview speech behavior under conditions of endogenously-present and exogenously-induced motivational states. *Journal of Clinical Psychology, 26,* 141-148.

McCornack, S. A. (1992). Information manipulation theory. *Communication Monographs, 59,* 1-16.

McCornack, S. A., & Levine, T. R. (1990). When lovers become leary: The relationship between suspicion and accuracy in detecting deception. *Communication Monographs, 57,* 219-230.

McCornack, S. A., Levine, T. R., Solowcsuk, K., Torres, H. I., & Campbell, D. M. (1992). When the alteration of information is viewed as deception: An empirical test of information manipulation theory. *Communication Monographs, 59,* 17-29.

McCornack, S. A., & Parks, M. R. (1986). Deception detection and relational development: The other side of trust. In M. L. McLaughlin (Ed.), *Communication yearbook
9* (pp. 377-389). Beverly Hills, CA: Sage.

McCroskey, J. C. (1966). Scales for the measurement of ethos. *Speech Monographs, 33,*
65-72.

Miller, G. R. (1983). Telling it like it isn't and not telling it like it is: Some thoughts on
deceptive communication. In J. I. Sisco (Ed.), *The Jensen lectures: Contemporary
communication studies* (pp. 91-116). Tampa: University of South Florida.

Miller, G. R., Bauchner, J. E., Hocking, J. E., Fontes, N. E., Kaminski, E. P., & Brandt,
D. R. (1981). ". . . and nothing but the truth": How well can observers detect
deceptive testimony? In B. D. Sales (Ed.), *Perspectives in law and psychology: Vol.
2. The jury, judicial, and trial process* (pp. 145-179). New York: Plenum.

Miller, G. R., & Burgoon, J. K. (1982). Factors affecting the assessments of witness
credibility. In N. Kerr & R. M. Bray (Eds.), *The psychology of the courtroom* (pp.
169-194). New York: Academic Press.

Miller, G. R., deTurck, M. A., & Kalbfleisch, P. J. (1983). Self-monitoring, rehearsal, and
deceptive communication. *Human Communication Research, 10,* 97-117.

Miller, G. R., Mongeau, P. A., & Sleight, C. (1984, June). *Fudging with friends and lying
to lovers: Deceptive communication in interpersonal relationships.* Paper presented
at the Second International Conference on Personal Relationships, Madison, WI.

Miller, G. R., Mongeau, P. A., & Sleight, C. (1986). Fudging with friends and lying to
lovers: Deceptive communication in interpersonal relationships. *Journal of Social
and Personal Relationships, 3,* 495-512.

Miller, G. R., Sleight, C., & deTurck, M. A. (1989). Arousal and attribution: Are the
behavioral cues monospecific? In C. V. Roberts & K. W. Watson (Eds.), *Interpersonal communication processes: Original essays* (pp. 273-291). New Orleans and
Scottsdale, AZ: Spectra and Gorsuch Scarisbrick.

Miller, G. R., & Steinberg, M. (1975). *Between people: A new analysis of interpersonal
communication.* Chicago: Science Research Associates.

Motley, M. (1974). Acoustical correlates of lies. *Western Speech, 38,* 81-87.

Nisbett, R., & Ross, L. (1980). *Human inference: Strategies and shortcomings of social
judgment.* Englewood Cliffs, NJ: Prentice-Hall.

O'Hair, H. D., Cody, M. J., & McLaughlin, M. L. (1981). Prepared lies, spontaneous lies,
Machiavellianism, and nonverbal communication. *Human Communication Research,
7,* 325-339.

Preston, I. L. (1989). The Federal Trade Commission's identification of implications as
constituting deceptive advertising. *University of Cincinnati Law Review, 57,* 1243-
1310.

Raskin, D. C., & Esplin, P. W. (1991). Assessment of children's statements of sexual
abuse. In J. Doris (Ed.), *The suggestibility of children's recollections: Implications
for eyewitness testimony* (pp. 153-164). Washington, DC: American Psychological
Association.

Richards, J. I. (1990). *Deceptive advertising: Behavioral study of a legal concept.*
Hillsdale, NJ: Lawrence Erlbaum.

Riggio, R. E., & Friedman, H. S. (1983). Individual differences and cues to deception.
Journal of Personality and Social Psychology, 45, 899-915.

Shulman, G. (1973). *An experimental study of the effects of receiver sex, communicator sex, and warning on the ability of receivers to detect deception.* Unpublished master's thesis, Department of Communication, Purdue University.

Silverman, L. J., Rivera, A. N., & Tedeschi, J. T. (1979). Transgression compliance: Guilt, negative affect, or impression management? *Journal of Social Psychology, 108,* 57-62.

Snyder, M. (1974). Self-monitoring of expressive behavior. *Journal of Personality and Social Psychology, 30,* 526-537.

Sparks, G. G., & Greene, J. O. (1992). On the validity of nonverbal indicators as measures of physiological arousal: A response to Burgoon, Kelley, Newton, & Kelley-Dyreson. *Human Communication Research, 18,* 445-471.

Steller, M., & Koehnken, G. (1989). Criteria-based statement analysis. In D. C. Raskin (Ed.), *Psychological methods in criminal investigation and evidence* (pp. 217-245). New York: Springer.

Steller, M., Wellershaus, P., & Wolfe, T. (1988, June). *Empirical validation of criteria based content analysis.* Paper presented at the meeting of the NATO Advanced Study Institute on Credibility Assessment, Maratea, Italy.

Stiff, J. B., Corman, S. R., & Raghavendra, S. (1991, May). *Exploring the process of deception detection.* Paper presented at the annual meeting of the International Communication Association, Chicago.

Stiff, J. B., Corman, S. R., Snider, E., & Krizek, R. (1992, May). *Individual differences and changes in nonverbal behavior: Unmasking the changing faces of deception.* Paper presented at the annual meeting of the International Communication Association, Miami.

Stiff, J. B., Kim, H. J., & Ramesh, C. (1992). Truth biases and aroused suspicion in relational deception. *Communication Research, 19,* 326-345.

Stiff, J. B., & Miller, G. R. (1986). "Come to think of it . . .": Interrogative probes, deceptive communication, and deception detection. *Human Communication Research, 12,* 339-357.

Stiff, J. B., Miller, G. R., Sleight, C., Mongeau, P. A., Garlick, R., & Rogan, R. (1989). Explanations for visual cue primacy in judgments of honesty and deceit. *Journal of Personality and Social Psychology, 56,* 555-564.

Taylor, S. E. (1981). The interface of cognitive and social psychology. In J. Harvey (Ed.), *Cognition, social behavior, and the environment* (pp. 189-212). Hillsdale, NJ: Lawrence Erlbaum.

Taylor, S. E., & Fiske, S. T. (1978). Salience, attention, and attribution: Top of the head phenomena. In L. Berkowitz (Ed.), *Advances in experimental social psychology* (Vol. 11, pp. 249-288). New York: Academic Press.

Taylor, S. E., & Thompson, S. C. (1982). Stalking the elusive "vividness" effect. *Psychological Review, 89,* 155-181.

Tversky, A., & Kahneman, D. (1974). Judgment under uncertainty: Heuristics and biases. *Science, 185,* 1124-1131.

Undeutsch, U. (1989). The development of statement reality analysis. In J. C. Yuille (Ed.), *Credibility assessment* (pp. 101-120). Dordrecht, The Netherlands: Kluwer.

Wade, W. M., & Orne, M. T. (1981). Cognitive, social, and personality processes in the physiological detection of deception. In L. Berkowitz (Ed.), *Advances in experimental social psychology* (Vol. 14, pp. 61-106). New York: Academic Press.

Wagner, H., & Pease, K. (1976). The verbal communication of inconsistency between attitudes held and attitudes expressed. *Journal of Personality, 44,* 1-16.

Wegener, H. (1989). The present state of statement analysis. In J. C. Yuille (Ed.), *Credibility assessment* (pp. 121-134). Dordrecht, The Netherlands: Kluwer.

Wright, P. (1981). Cognitive responses to mass media advocacy. In R. Petty, T. M. Ostrom, & T. C. Brock (Eds.), *Cognitive responses to persuasion* (pp. 263-282). Hillsdale, NJ: Lawrence Erlbaum.

Wyer, R. S., & Srull, T. K. (1981). Category accessibility: Some theoretical and empirical issues concerning the processing of social stimulus information. In E. T. Higgins, C. P. Herman, & M. P. Zanna (Eds.), *Social cognition: The Ontario symposium* (Vol. 1, pp. 161-197). Hillsdale, NJ: Lawrence Erlbaum.

Zimbardo, P., Snyder, M., Thomas, J., Gold, A., & Gurwitz, S. (1970). Modifying the impact of persuasive communications with external distraction. *Journal of Personality and Social Psychology, 16,* 669-680.

Zuckerman, M., Amidon, M. D., Bishop, S. E., & Pomerantz, S. D. (1982). Face and tone of voice in the communication of deception. *Journal of Personality and Social Psychology, 43,* 347-357.

Zuckerman, M., DeFrank, R. S., Hall, J. A., Larrance, D. T., & Rosenthal, R. (1979). Facial and vocal cues of deception and honesty. *Journal of Experimental Social Psychology, 15,* 378-396.

Zuckerman, M., DePaulo, B. M., & Rosenthal, R. (1981). Verbal and nonverbal communication of deception. In L. Berkowitz (Ed.), *Advances in experimental social psychology* (Vol. 14, pp. 1-59). New York: Academic Press.

Zuckerman, M., & Driver, R. (1985). Telling lies: Verbal and nonverbal correlates of deception. In A. W. Siegman & S. Feldstein (Eds.), *Nonverbal communication: An integrated perspective* (pp. 129-147). Hillsdale, NJ: Lawrence Erlbaum.

Zuckerman, M., Koestner, R., & Alton, A. O. (1984). Learning to detect deception. *Journal of Personality and Social Psychology, 46,* 519-528.

Author Index

Allen, V. L., 21
Allport, G. W., 17
Alton, A. O., 79-81, 117
Amidon, M. D., 76
Apple, W., 76

Bargh, J. A., 113
Bauchner, J. E., 21, 24, 26, 42-44, 72, 73, 83, 97
Bavelas, J. B., x, 20, 21, 48, 52, 106, 112
Berger, C. R., 86
Berlo, D. K., 19
Bishop, S. E., 76
Black, A., x, 20, 21, 48, 52, 106, 112
Bok, S., 1, 5, 15, 20, 23, 34, 113, 115, 111
Boychuk, T. D., 111
Brandt, D. R., 24, 26, 43, 44, 70, 72, 73, 78-80, 97
Buller, D. B., 25, 92, 98, 104
Burgoon, J. K., 55

Campbell, D. M., 107, 112
Chaiken, S., 73, 75, 113
Chappell, M. N., 52

Chovil, N., x, 20, 21, 48, 52, 106, 112
Cody, M. J., 39, 41, 50, 51, 55, 56, 60, 63, 66, 85, 86, 87, 112
Collins, R. L., 73
Comadena, M. E., 1, 20, 44, 97, 98
Comstock, J., 25, 92, 98, 104
Crowne, D., 25

Davis, T., 61, 86
DeFrank, R. S., 21
Dennis, H. S., 21, 39, 50, 51, 53, 56, 74
DePaulo, B. M., 55, 56, 61, 69, 70, 86, 112
deTurck, M. A., 24, 26, 43, 44, 54, 60, 61, 88, 89, 103, 111, 117
Devin-Sheehan, L., 21
DeVito, J. A., 67
Dillard, J. P., 86
Driver, R., 55, 61, 62, 112
Donohue, W. A., 93

Eck, M., 18, 20, 23
Ekman, P., x, 21, 24, 51, 69, 70, 83
Elliott, G. C., 87
Esplin, P. W., 110, 111

Exline, R. E., 26, 43, 44

Feldman, R. S., x, 21
Fiske, S. T., 75
Fontes, N. E., 97
Foster, M., 39, 50, 51, 55, 56, 60, 63, 66, 86, 87, 112
Friedman, H. S., 66
Friesen, W. V., x, 21, 24, 51, 70, 83

Gold, A., 72
Gouldner, A. W., 14
Greene J. O., 86, 87, 112
Grice, H. P., 106, 107, 109, 112
Gumpert, P., 26, 43, 44
Gurwitz, S., 72
Gustafson, L. A., 52

Hall, J. A., 21
Harszlak, J. J., 117
Hart, R. P., 21, 39, 50, 51, 53, 56, 74
Hecht, M. L., 67
Hickey, C. B., 26, 43, 44
Hocking, J. E., 21, 24, 42, 70, 72, 78-80, 83
Hundaker, F. G., 25

Insko, C. A., 72

Jackson, R. H., 85
Janzen, J. C., 66
Jones, E. E., 23

Kahneman, D., 75, 98
Kalbfleisch, P. J., 69, 80
Kaminski, E. P., 21, 24, 42, 72, 83, 97
Kaplan, E. P., 26, 43
Knapp, 1, 20, 21, 39, 50, 51, 53, 56, 74
Koehnken, G., 110
Koestner, R., 79-81, 117
Krauss, R. M., 76
Kraut, R., 50, 51, 58, 64, 66, 69, 70

Lanier, K., 61, 86
Larrance, D. T., 21
Lassiter, G. D., 61
Lemert, J. B., 19
Lennox, R. D., 87
Levine, 35, 45, 107, 112
Littlepage, G., E., 24, 85, 86
Locke, E. A., 33
Ludwig, A. M., 20
Lykken, D. T., 51-53

Maier, N. R. F., 53, 66, 72, 73
Manaugh, T. S., 85
Marlow, D., 25
Marston, P. J., 39, 50, 51, 55, 56, 60, 63, 66, 86, 87, 112
Matarazzo, J. D., 85
McCornack, S. A., 14, 35, 45, 98, 106, 107, 110, 112
McCroskey, J. C., 19
McLaughlin, M. L., 85
Mertz, R. J., 19
Miller, G. R., 13-15, 20, 21, 24, 26, 28, 29, 31, 36, 42-44, 46, 54, 50, 54, 55, 61, 70, 72, 73, 78-80, 83, 88, 89, 96-98, 103, 111, 117
Mongeau, P. A., 14, 15, 46, 78, 97, 98
Morency, N., 76
Motley, M., 21
Mullett, J., x, 20, 21, 48, 52, 106, 112

Nisbett, R., 73

O'Hair, H. D., 41, 85, 86, 87, 112
Orne, M. T., 51, 52
O'Sullivan, M., 69

Parks, M. R., 14, 35, 45, 98
Pease, K., 51
Pineault, M. A., 24, 84, 85
Poe, D., 69
Pomerantz, S. D., 76
Postman, L. J., 17
Pratto, F., 113

Preston, I. L., 7-9

Raskin, D. C., 110, 111
Richards, J. I., 9, 10
Riggio, R., E., 66
Rivera, A. N., 91
Rosenthal, R., 21, 55, 56, 61, 69, 70, 86, 112
Ross, L., 73

Scrull, T. K., 75
Shulman, G., 26
Silverman, L. J., 91
Sleight, C., 14, 15, 46, 54, 78, 97, 98
Slovic, 75
Snyder, M., 72, 87
Solowcsuk, K., 107, 112
Sparks, G. G., 112
Steinberg, M., 13, 36, 96
Steller, M., 110, 111
Stiff, J. B., 26, 35, 42-45, 48, 50, 51, 56-58, 60, 63-65, 68, 74, 75, 91, 92, 93, 98, 103, 105, 106, 109, 110, 112, 115, 116
Stone, J. I., 61
Strzyzewski, K. D., 25, 92, 98, 104

Taylor, S. E., 73, 75
Tedeschi, J. T., 91
Texter, l. A., 117
Thibaut, J., 26, 43, 44

Thomas, J., 72
Thompson, S. C., 73
Thurber, J., 72, 73
Torres, H. I., 107, 112
Turnbull, W., 72
Tversky, A., 75, 98

Undeutsch, U., 110

Wade, W. M., 51, 52
Wagner, H., 51
Wegener, H., 110
Wellershaus, P., 111
Wenzel, C., 76
Wiens, A. N., 85
Winton, W., 76
Wolfe, R. N., 87
Wolfe, T., 111
Wood, S. C., 73
Wortman, C., 23
Wright, P., 73
Wyer, R. S., 75

Yandell, B., 72
Yen, C., 86, 87, 112

Zimbardo, P., 72
Zuckerman, M., 21, 55, 56, 61, 62, 69, 70, 76, 79-81, 86, 112, 117

Subject Index

Anticipation of deception, 35, 41, 43, 45-47

Arousal theory, 52-54, 84-86, 112

Baseline information, 78-80, 96-97

Cognitive heuristics, 75, 98, 101, 113

Cognitive theory, 55, 84-87, 113

Consequences of detection,
  economic, 34
  general 34, 67, 80
  political, 4, 5, 36
  relational, 14-15, 34, 37, 44-45

Conversational norms (maxims), 106-110, 112

Cooperative principle, 106, 110

Deception code, 66, 81

Deceptive contexts,
  advertising, 6-12
  child abuse interviews, 48, 104, 110-111
  interpersonal relationships, 12-15, 36-37, 98-99
  political, 2-6, 36

Deceptive judgments,
  nonverbal correlates of, 45-46, 65-66
  verbal correlates of, 46, 65-66

Deceptive tactics,
  apparent self-disclosure, 13
  duping delight, 30
  in advertising, 7-12
  ingratiation, 23
  lying, 4, 6
  white lies, 14, 23

Defining deception,
  as persuasion, 28-31
  as transactional process, 38, 41, 43-45, 48
  communicator intent, 19-23, 52
  discourse related factors, 19-22
  vs. leveling effect, 17
  vs. lying, 22
  vs. message inaccuracies, 18-22, 52

Detection accuracy,
  among professionals, 69
  definition of, 68
  idiosyncratic behavior, 78-80
  implications of, 69-71
  information processing errors, 71-78
  interrogative probes, 95
  mode of presentation, 73
  planned vs. spontaneous deception, 84-90

relational deception, 97-98
Distraction hypothesis, 72-75

Ethics,
    of deception, 1-2
    of deception research, 27, 38, 41, 43-44,
        49, 113-117
    of Exline procedure, 44
    of honesty, 13-14
Exline procedure, 26-27, 43-44, 54, 65, 91,
    103, 105

Factual deception, 25-27, 83-84, 99
Federal Trade Commission, 7, 10
File drawer problem, 59-60

Idiosyncratic behavior, 78-81
Information processing errors, 71-78
Interaction analysis, 47-49, 105-109
Interrogative probes,
    detection accuracy, 95
    nonverbal behavior, 91-95
    types of, 93-95
    verbal behavior, 91-95, 106-109

Leakage hypothesis, 51

Meta-analysis, 61-63, 69
Motivation,
    to deceive, 24, 27, 30, 34, 41-43, 45, 103
    to detect deception, 30, 34-35, 37, 41,
        43-46

Nonverbal behavior,
    arousal, 21, 52-54, 84
    associated with deception, 45-46, 59, 61-62
    associated with deceptive judgments, 65-66
    coding of, 56
    cognitive effort, 55, 84-86

deception-induced arousal, 54
deceptive intent, 21
    emphasis on, 76-77
    investigation of, 55-57
    motivation to deceive, 62
    planning, 62, 86-87

Planned deception, 61-62, 84-90,
    and self-monitoring, 87-80
Polygraph exams, 51-53, 103
Principle of veracity, 34

Reaction assessments, 42-43
Relational deception,
    baseline information, 96-97
    detection accuracy, 97-98
    truth bias, 98-99
Relational interviews, 44-45
Research designs,
    categories of 39-49
    criteria for evaluating, 37-40
    essential features of, 34-36
    factual deception, 25-27, 41-42
    generalizability, 32-37, 43
    importance of differences among, 60-
        61
    in natural settings, 102-103
    self-feeling deception, 24-25, 42

Sanctioned deception, 3, 36, 41-43, 47, 103
Self-feeling deception, 24-25, 83-84, 99
Self-monitoring,
    definition of, 87
    planned deception, 87-90
Simulated interviews, 45-46
Situational familiarity hypothesis, 75-77
Statement validity analysis, 110-111
Survey interviews, 46-47
Suspicion, 35, 45, 98-99

Time series analysis, 105-106

Truth bias, 35, 98-99

Uninterrupted message presentations, 39, 41-42

Veracity judgments, *see* Deceptive judgments

Verbal behavior,
    associated with deception, 61-65, 106
    associated with deceptive judgments, 65-66
    child abuse interviews, 110-111
    cognitive effort, 55
    holistic estimates of, 58
    investigation of, 56-59

About the Authors

Gerald R. Miller is a University Distinguished Professor at Michigan State University. He is the author or editor of 11 books and more than 150 articles on interpersonal communication and related areas. He is a past President of the International Communication Association, the founding editor of *Human Communication Research,* and a former editor of *Communication Monographs.*

James B. Stiff is an Associate Professor of Communication at Arizona State University. His teaching and research interests include interpersonal communication and social influence. He has authored 20 published articles and book chapters on these topics in journals such as *Human Communication Research, Communication Research, Communication Monographs,* and *The Journal of Personality and Social Psychology* and he is presently writing a book on persuasive communication.